# NOTHING TO IT
Reading Freud as a Philosopher

# FIGURES OF THE UNCONSCIOUS 17

# NOTHING TO IT

## Reading Freud as a Philosopher

Emmanuel Falque

*Translation by*
*Robert Vallier & William L. Connelly*

LEUVEN UNIVERSITY PRESS

Authorized translation from the French language edition *"Ca" n'a rien a voir*
published by Les éditions du Cerf, Paris.
© 2018 French language edition by Les éditions du Cerf, Paris.
© 2020 English language edition by Leuven University Press / Universitaire Pers
Leuven / Presses Universitaires de Louvain. Minderbroedersstraat 4, B-3000
Leuven (Belgium).

ISBN 978 94 6270 223 3
e-ISBN 978 94 6166 321 4
D/2020/1869/12
NUR: 730
https://doi.org/10.11116/9789461663214

Cover design: Daniel Benneworth-Gray
Lay-out: Friedemann Vervoort

**GPRC**
Guaranteed
Peer Reviewed
Content
www.gprc.be

For Sabine Fos-Falque,
psychoanalyst

We are mistaken in regarding our intelligence
as an independent force and in overlooking
its dependence on emotional life.

Sigmund Freud,
*Thoughts for the Times
on War and Death*
November 1914

# Table of Contents

Foreword by Philippe Van Haute          13

Preface          19

Opening Act
Philosophizing in psychoanalysis          23
    *The doctrine of experience*          24
    *The other Rubicon*          25
    *The backlash*          28

Introduction
Go take a look          35

Chapter One
Keep moving, nothing to see          39
    *The end of the Enlightenment*          40
    *Toward another paradigm*          42
    *Collapse of the system*          44

Chapter Two

Beware of it                                49

   *Conceiving the inconceivable*        50

   *The disillusion of psychoanalysis*    52

   *Primitive man*                        53


Chapter Three

It's not nothing                            59

   *The drive at the frontier*            60

   *Rooting in the organic*               62

   *Presence and resistance*              65


Chapter Four

What is it?                                 69

   *A disturbing uncanny*                 69

   *Death and repetition*                 70

   *The anorganic*                        72


Chapter Five

It concerns me                              79

   *Being lived*                          80

   *The knight of the Id*                 81

   *Being there for something*            82

Chapter Six

It touches me                                    85

*Where the Id was*                               85
*The draining of the Zuyderzee*                  87
*The great cavalcade*                            89


Conclusion

What's God have to do with it?                   93

*For the salvation of the Id*                    93
*Apart from it*                                  94
*The realm of the Id*                            95


Epilogue

Regarding all of it                              99


Notes                                            103


Bibliography                                     123


Index rerum                                      131


Index nominum                                    135

# Foreword

Husserl's *Logische Untersuchungen* and Freud's *The Interpretation of Dreams* were both published in 1900. Each of these books changed the intellectual landscape of their time by respectively founding two new disciplines. In the years following their publication, Freud and Husserl developed these disciplines further without even mentioning each other. It is only after the disappearance of the founders that it became clear to their followers that both disciplines might benefit in many ways from a sustained dialogue between them. Ever since that time, the development of both psychoanalysis and phenomenology has been intertwined in such an essential way that one might wonder whether the development of one discipline can be properly understood without taking the other into account. Not only was psychoanalysis, in one way or another, a reference point for many phenomenologists, but it was especially in the French context that phenomenology also played a crucial role in post-Freudian thinking.

However, the relation between phenomenology and psychoanalysis has not always been easy. Too often, philosophers claimed that their discipline was able to articulate in a much clearer way the psychoanalytic insights that were of interest to them. Indeed, according to these authors these insights were covered up in a scientistic language that betrayed their true nature. Hence, phenomenology had to unearth the philosophical essence of psychoanalytic metapsychology and render it in a more appropriate, phenomenological vocabulary. In this view phenomenology was, in a certain sense, the true destiny of psychoanalytic metapsychology. It is thus no wonder that psychoanalysts felt misrecognized and unjustifiably reduced to a footnote in the history of philosophy. They claimed, on the contrary, that without thoroughly acquainting oneself with 'psychoanalytic experience'—that is, without becoming a psychoanalyst oneself—no true understanding of psychoanalysis is possible. Psychoanalysis is not a theory (*Weltanschauung*), but a praxis. As a result, philosophy has no authority in the psychoanalytic field. In this way the relation—but wasn't it also quite often a non-relation?—between the two disciplines turned into a dialogue of the deaf.

It would be a great injustice to many authors working at the intersection of psychoanalysis and phenomenology if we were to reduce the history of the encounter between psychoanalysis and phenomenology to the alternative that I have just outlined. Rather, this alternative has been like a cloud that in one way or another casts its shadow over the dialogue at hand. It reminds us of what is at stake in this dialogue. Emmanuel Falque turns towards Merleau-Ponty to elucidate these stakes for philosophy: "There are not *two kinds of knowledge*, but *two different degrees of clarification of the same knowledge*. Psychology and philosophy *are nourished by the same phenomena*; it is only that the problems become more formalized at the philosophical level.... When philosophers wish to place reason above the vicissitudes of history they cannot purely and simply forget what psychology, sociology, ethnography, history, and psychiatry have taught us about the conditioning of human behaviour."[1]

But Emmanuel Falque wants to go further than this. In his philosophical reflections on the relation between phenomenology and psychoanalysis, he does not only want to do justice to psychoanalysis, but is more concretely concerned with the ways in which psychoanalysis contributes or should contribute to changing the course of contemporary phenomenology. Here again it is Merleau-Ponty who leads the way. Or rather, it is Emmanuel Falque who suspects a profound and instructive parallel between the evolution of Freud's thinking from the first topography "to the plunge into obscurity and the Id's resistance in the second topography," and the evolution of Merleau-Ponty's philosophy from the early works to the *Visible and the Invisible*. Whereas Freud's early theories would be completely oriented towards consciousness (rendering the unconscious libidinal representations conscious), the development of a model of a psychic structure comprised of the id, ego and super-ego in the later works would imply a re-centering of Freudian thinking—a Freudian metaphysics?—around the 'It', the body and the (death)drives that are beyond any representation or meaning whatsoever. In an analogous, or rather parallel fashion, the evolution of Merleau-Ponty's thinking from *Phenomenology of Perception* to the *Prose of the World* and the *Visible and the Invisible* would oblige us to break with the primacy of the visual (the paradigm of consciousness), which is instead replaced by the model of touching that points beyond the ideal of transparency and more radically towards a 'below of sense' that transcends the couple of sense and non-sense.

In this way, the essential proximity—a proximity that can never become a fusion or an identity—of psychoanalysis and phenomenology that Emmanuel Falque wants to understand, progressively takes form. The following passage that Falque takes from Merleau-Ponty's Preface to Hesnard's *L'Oeuvre de Freud* shows what it is about and in what ways it differs from the false alternative from which we started: "This phenomenology which *descends into its own underground* is converging more than ever with Freudian research.... The accord of phenomenology and of psychoanalysis should not be understood to consist in phenomenology's saying clearly what psychoanalysis had said obscurely. On the contrary, it is by what phenomenology implies or unveils as its limits—by its *latent content* or its *unconscious*— that it is in consonance with psychoanalysis."[2] Just as Freud was forced to leave the ideals of the Enlightenment behind him, so phenomenology can no longer exclusively stick to intentionality and its continuous search for signification. Both phenomenology and psychoanalysis can be changed by what the other reveals without one being reduced to the other.

This brings me to one of the most original aspects of Falque's reflections. He explains how certain disillusions of the First World War were at the basis of a reformulation of Freudian psychoanalysis. Freud no longer placed consciousness and meaning at the centre of his metapsychology. This shift is most clearly expressed in his *Beyond the Pleasure Principle* (and the texts from the same period in which some of its essential aspects are further developed) that was first published in 1920. One can discuss Falque's historical contextualisation of these texts, but it is at the same time clear that placing them at the centre of a dialogue with phenomenology gives to them an importance that does justice to their explicit metaphysical pretentions. The introduction of the death drives (Freud almost always uses the plural here) that works in silence—that concerns me, without offering anything to be seen ('Ca me regarde d'autant plus que ça ne donne rien à voir')—once and for all breaks with the horizon of possible intelligibility.

"But what is 'it' then?" asks Emmanuel Falque. 'It' is intrinsically linked to death and the anorganic that is the ultimate goal of the drive of which 'it' consists. But one should not think that this goal is something that is just lying in front of us. Rather, the notion of 'death drives' indicates a principle of inertia that essentially inhabits our lives and characterizes 'it,' so to speak. Something in us does not want to change or, what comes down to the same thing, it doesn't want to live. The organic elasticity of the drive that Freud is talking about, and which Falque brings to our attention, implies that the drive essentially wants to return to its previous (anorganic) state. Life doesn't exist without a refusal to go along with it. This means that something in us is always already dead. This death is not a possibility of *Dasein* as Heidegger claimed in *Being and Time.* It is, on the contrary, beyond meaning and possibility. It is something neutral and outside of any possible signification (and which resists it, too).

But Falque is right to remind us that all of this didn't have much importance if it wouldn't at the same time concern us. In the texts that follow *Beyond the Pleasure Principle* Freud deepens the relation between the id and the ego that can no longer be thought *or* experienced as the master in its own house: "With *Ego and the Id* (1923), after the *Thoughts for the Times on War and Death* (1914), *The Drives and their Vicissitudes* (1915),

*The Uncanny* (1920), and *Beyond the Pleasure Principle* (1920), we gradually and almost helplessly participate in a sort of 'falling apart of the ego's house,' (…)I gradually come to feel uncanny, like 'a stranger in my own home' (*das Unheimliche*)" (Falque, 81). Indeed, the ego is not standing over and against the id. It is, quite on the contrary, part of the id as Freud clearly states in *The Ego and the Id*. Falque concludes: "Definitively warned against all false bids or temptations of the impermeability of the psychic spheres, the psychoanalyst gradually recognizes their instability and sees how we are 'engraved by the Id' in the whole of our being. The world is made of 'chiasm,' 'transition,' 'interlacing' and 'entanglement' according to a lesson that Merleau-Ponty himself probably received from Freud" (Falque, 88). In other words, psychoanalysis obliges phenomenology to explore its own limits—and the way in which we relate to them—that are also the limits of signification as such.

*Nothing to It* is a short book on the relation between psychoanalysis and phenomenology. This topic has been discussed by a great number of philosophers and psychoanalysts ever since psychoanalysis came into being. Clearly, it still leaves many questions open but it also very clearly gives an original and new approach to this problem. Not only does this approach respect the independence of both disciplines while at the same time describing their chiastic relation, but in placing *Beyond the Pleasure Principle* at the centre of its reflections it also highlights, once again, the philosophical potential and importance of this enigmatic text. Both philosophers and psychoanalysts should be able to appreciate this move.

*Philippe Van Haute*
*Radboud University, Nijmegen, The Netherlands*

# Preface

Philosophy, especially in the case of phenomenology, cannot remain sequestered in its own discipline. Philosophers who are too self-satisfied—whether through pride, condescension, or self-sufficiency—are in danger of autarchy. The time is long past when phenomenology still played the game of exteriority, at least with respect to the human sciences, whether linguistics, cultural anthropology, or psychoanalysis. Surely the "short cut" today takes precedence over the "long road," that is, the lifeworld (*Lebenswelt*) takes precedence over the endless detour through cultural mediations. That is a point to which we cannot return. Yet at the time Paul Ricœur, as well as Maurice Merleau-Ponty, Jacques Derrida, Gilles Deleuze, or Michel Henry had already opened the path for a real dialogue between philosophy and psychoanalysis, which today is closed off or forgotten—either because of an ontic drift for some (philosophers and phenomenologists) or because of a negation of praxis for others (psychoanalysts and the inheritors of psychological practice). Nevertheless Freud can and should be read today anew *as a philosopher*, if we are to free ourselves of the ontic condemnation of him (by phenomenologists) or of a kind of terrorism of experience (by psychologists).

The "backlash of psychoanalysis onto phenomenology"—
and not solely that of theology on phenomenology—has not
yet fully borne fruit. A supplemental step must now be taken.
Although Paul Ricœur effectively began an "open" dialogue with
psychoanalysis, it must still be accomplished fully, even directed in
a different way. It is entirely possible that the "excess of meaning"
in contemporary philosophy—interpretation (hermeneutics) or
signification (phenomenology)—has something to learn from
psychoanalysis itself. Ricœur and other philosophers remained
within the horizon of the "signified," Michel Henry insisted on
the unquestioned possibility of experience. Instead, we must
now question the limits of hermeneutics and phenomenology
*ad intra*, as Merleau-Ponty did in his later works, insofar as
an attack *ad extra* of psychoanalysis must make us wonder
about the *a priori* of *meaning* that is continually being posited.
History always goes on when one falsely believes it to be fully
accomplished. There are many attacks, including against
psychoanalysis, which would make us believe that it no longer
has the cultural means for dialogue, thus setting it aside as an
exercise reserved only for a few specialists. This *short treatise*
therefore aims to confront the two disciplines of philosophy
"and" psychoanalysis with one another once again. If it cannot
manage to open the debate differently, then at least it might
prevent it from being closed down definitively.

Thus, to say that there is "*nothing to it*" does not mean that
there are no relations between philosophy and psychoanalysis,
quite the contrary. It is also not about claiming that in their aims
and practices neither would be unable to escape their respective
boxes. Rather, "nothing to it" [*Ça n'a rien à voir*] means, strictly
speaking, that the Id [*Ça*], *is not seen* [*ne se voit pas*]—because it
precisely never becomes defined as a "phenomenon" and even

definitively escapes any horizon of phenomenality. The Freudian Id is not seen, but it "looks" at me and "concerns" me [*il me "regarde"*]. It is the task of the philosopher here to let it simply "be there," not to challenge it but simply to permit it to exist. This might allow us to question the limits of a phenomenology that wants to embrace everything with impunity. This is no longer a matter of presence as "remainder" (counter-phenomenon), but of presence as "resistance" (the extra-phenomenal). In the first case, the remainder is no more than a relic of the excess of the revealed. In the second case, the very possibility of unveiling is annihilated. Trauma suppresses the very capacity to "experience" or "feel" it. Perhaps the Freudian Id wants to lead us to this radical experience.

By passing from the first to the second topography, Freud progressively gave up on the original ideal of the Enlightenment (*Aufklärung*), the paradigm of a controlled scientificity, with its duly demarcated borders. The Id, the ego and the superego gradually won out over the unconscious, preconscious, and conscious, because on the one hand, psychoanalytic practice itself required it (borderline cases), and on the other hand, certain historical circumstances (such as World War I) and personal events (the death of his daughter Sophie and his jaw cancer) could not but lead there. It is when the system "cracks" that we can measure its capacity: not necessarily for reconstruction but for living differently the Chaos of existence that can no longer be so easily hidden. This is what this essay wants to undertake anew, *philosophically* at first but also in direct dialogue with psychoanalysis.

*Mettray, France*
*March 1ˢᵗ, 2018*

# Philosophizing in psychoanalysis

> In spite of serious misunderstandings, which I do not underestimate, *a philosopher*, as *a philosopher*, is capable of understanding psychoanalytic theory and even in part psychoanalytic experience.[1]

There is certainly something surprising about Paul Ricœur's acknowledgment in *The Conflict of Interpretations* (1969)—at least to those who practice psychoanalysis. Nothing assures us that it is consistent, or even appropriate, for a philosopher *to pass through* psychoanalysis, since "passing," at least in this context, seems to mean experiencing rather than understanding or theorizing. Analysis is often like religion: some "have experience," others do not—and only the former can talk about it. One enters psychoanalysis as one enters religion or takes the veil: only those committed to it know what it's like, and recognize each other as peers within the same community.

## *The doctrine of experience*

By leaning on Paul Ricœur or even from personal experience, we might thus say that it is at least possible to clear the space in which a discipline (psychoanalysis), and even its author (Freud), can be studied independently of the practice underlying it. The philosopher's viewpoint does not deny experience but sees it in a new light—not by excluding it but by treating it *differently*. The quest for a certain objectivity or the use of the text as sole datum confers a scientific weight on the work that psychoanalysis itself has always demanded from its beginnings:

> And so I say that Freud can be read just as our colleagues and teachers read Plato, Descartes, and Kant…. This *reference of doctrine to an experience* … does this reference not completely separate Freud from the thinkers and philosophers cited above? I still think that *such an objection is not invincible* and that the reading of Freud poses no different problem from the reading of Plato, Descartes, and Kant and can claim the same type of objectivity.[2]

So let us say it once and for all but without really daring to admit to it because this kind of caution is always interpreted as the "resistance" of whoever formulates it: Doesn't this constant reference to the "doctrine of experience," in Ricœur's words, sometimes produce (at least among those who profess it) a kind of "terrorism of experience" in psychoanalytic practice, sort of like the religious practice that insists that whoever has not undergone it, *really* has no right to speak about it? It had better not—far from it—occur to anyone (and even less to the psychoanalyst, at least if well trained) that *everyone* must participate in the experience of therapy. The cure requires a mode of "pathology," which is not only basic "curiosity." Wanting to know oneself otherwise or differently does not necessarily impose introspection except as medication, which is why psychoanalytic practice cannot extend to the whole of a humanity that would have need of repression. Nevertheless, those who "practice" psychoanalysis continue to hold on to the cherished conviction—all the more powerful when it remains hidden or unacknowledged—that those who have *undergone it* are fundamentally different from those who have not risked its danger. When one knows "from experience" one often wrongly thinks—in the religious domain (conversion) as much as in the therapeutic (the cure)—that the truth is to be had *there*. One expects that others will finally allow themselves to be led, even in their own way, toward those unexpected depths where the self will be finally and completely renewed. No one knows the path with certainty but some think, or might think, that said path is *the* only way to climb or reach the summit. From this results a sort of "transcendence coming from above," as Maurice Merleau-Ponty said, even a kind of "condescension" that sometimes haunts spiritual behavior (for the spiritual director) just as it does psychoanalytic practice (for the therapist)—which can just as easily make one want to run away from it rather than seek it out.

### The other Rubicon

What, then, would a discourse "about" psychoanalysis be independently of its practice? Has not the hour now struck for us "to cross the other Rubicon *philosophically*," to question the "turn"—not merely of phenomenology toward theology, but this time also that of phenomenology toward psychoanalysis?[3] To be sure, attempts to do so have not been lacking in the past, if we recall the frontal attacks and debates that are today often forgotten—from Deleuze and Guattari's *Anti-Oedipus* (published in 1972 in response to the events of May 1968) to Derrida's 1996 book *Resistances of Psychoanalysis.* What is all the same surprising, with one, albeit qualified, exception (Michel Henry's *The Genealogy of Psychoanalysis*),[4] is the silence and even distancing often maintained today especially by French phenomenology with respect to psychoanalysis. It is as if the battle had already been fought, perhaps won, and as if their mutual ignorance had definitively demarcated borders that have become sealed between the henceforth separated disciplines.

There is only one exception and precursor in the French landscape—Maurice Merleau-Ponty, who, from the *Phenomenology of Perception* (1945) until his sudden death in 1961, had warned against this separation. As we note in the chapter on "The Body as Sexed Being": "It would be *a mistake to believe* that psychoanalysis, even for Freud, excludes the description of psychological motives and is opposed to the phenomenological method. Psychoanalysis has, on the contrary (and unwittingly), *contributed to developing the phenomenological method.*"[5] "Psychoanalysis has contributed" and might yet contribute further "to the development of the phenomenological method": have we listened to this sufficiently and are we in line with it or in the process of extending it? In a debate the next year with the Société française de philosophie (1946), Merleau-Ponty even insists on it, in explicit opposition to those who accuse him of having "already given too much room to psychology" (which had been reduced to the rank of an "ontic science" along with all the other human sciences since the publication of Heidegger's *Being and Time*):

> There are not *two kinds of knowledge*, but *two different degrees of clarification of the same knowledge*. Psychology and philosophy *are nourished by the same phenomena*; it is only that the problems become more formalized at the philosophical level... When philosophers wish to place reason above the vicissitudes of history they cannot purely and simply forget what psychology, sociology, ethnography, history, and psychiatry have taught us about the conditioning of human behavior.[6]

On the eve of his appointment to the chair in philosophy at the College de France (1952), rallying to Husserl's position (at least in recognizing a certain, however outmoded, anchoring in descriptive psychology) and against the Heideggerians (who only deny it), Merleau-Ponty argues that:

> We need neither *tear down the behavioral sciences* to lay the foundations of philosophy, nor *tear down philosophy* to lay the foundations of the behavioral sciences. *Every science secretes an ontology*; every ontology anticipates a body of *knowledge*. It is *up to us to come to terms* with this situation and see to it that both philosophy and science are possible.[7]

In short, we need not reconcile psychoanalysis and philosophy because in reality they have already been married for a long time. But we still have to nourish the link, and any fidelity demands not only self-denial, but instead a willingness to approach the other. To do this, one must also for oneself give up or at least change and no longer stick to the standards that have shaped us. Merleau-Ponty tells us in a 1951-52 course at the Sorbonne that "Scheler and Heidegger… *remain* opposed to the simplistic opposition of philosophy and the human sciences, of the *ontological*, as Heidegger said, and the *ontic*… an opposition that for Husserl, as we have seen, was only a point of departure."[8] Even better this same course on "The Human Sciences and Phenomenology" clearly invokes the idea of a "relation of intertwining or envelopment between psychology and phenomenology"—even of "encroachment" or "overlapping of two orders." The phenomenologist concludes with a new invitation to the study of psychoanalysis: "the logic of things had led Husserl to admit deeper relations," a "homogeneity," and even an "interlacing"—the key term in what will later become *The Visible and the Invisible.*[9] In short, it is good to go from phenomenology to psychoanalysis. Where some would have liked to believe wrongly in a war, in reality there is peace—or rather, a justice of the peace who avoids war by "exercising" both, albeit in a theoretical fashion, and leaves each to see what there is in the practice.

## *The backlash*

What kind of "backlash" does *psychoanalysis* produce in *phenomenology*, then, such that it "contributes to the development" and even to "modifying" or "changing the course" of phenomenology? We will distinguish in psychoanalysis two great moments or stages of fecundity, even of transformation, with respect to phenomenology. The first moment comes from Ricœur's 1965 book *Freud and Philosophy*, which is subtitled "An Essay on Interpretation." It sees in the earliest psychoanalytic theory one of the great authorities or even the principal source of the unfurling of hermeneutics. A certain affinity or even contemporaneity can be read implicitly between Freud's *Interpretation of Dreams* (1899), in developing a "theory of interpretation" based on symptom, phantasm, and signification, and that of Husserl's *Logical Investigations* (1900), in uncovering a "theory of the signified" linked to the "given" rather than to objectivity.[10] In short, there is no conflict between psychoanalysis and phenomenology in their respective origins, but only the necessity, at least in Ricœur's eyes, to radicalize the theory of "signification" (Husserl) with a theory of "interpretation" (Freud). To sum it up in a few words, even a leitmotif, first articulated by Husserl in his 1929 *Cartesian Meditations*, which serves today as the spearhead for any phenomenology, and perhaps also for psychoanalysis: "Its beginning is *the pure—and, so to speak, still mute—psychological experience*, which now must be made to utter its own sense with no adulteration."[11]

The second moment is drawn from Merleau-Ponty—not solely to mark the "affinity" between psychoanalysis and phenomenology, but rather to demonstrate how a certain "sharing of the shadow" or the "depths of obscurity" must also belong to phenomenology itself. Surely, at least in the *Phenomenology of Perception*, Merleau-Ponty agrees with Ricœur in taking the "signified" as the shared horizon of the two disciplines: "Psychoanalysis has, on the contrary (and unwittingly), contributed to developing the phenomenological method by claiming, as Freud puts it, that every human act "'*has a sense*'...."[12] But just one year later, in a 1946 interview with Émile Bréhier, he adds that: "The will to

apply reason *to what is taken as irrational* is a *progress for reason.*"[13]
This second "backlash" of psychoanalysis on phenomenology,
announced also in my own work, which I now seek to deepen,[14]
is in my view accomplished in the few pages of Merleau-Ponty's
magisterial preface to the first great monograph in France on the
founder of psychoanalysis, Hesnard's *L'Œuvre de Freud* (1960):

> This phenomenology which *descends into its own
> underground* is converging more than ever with
> Freudian research… The accord of phenomenology
> and of psychoanalysis should not be understood
> to consist in phenomenology's saying clearly what
> psychoanalysis had said obscurely. On the contrary,
> it is by what phenomenology implies or unveils as its
> limits—by its *latent content* or its *unconscious*—that
> it is in consonance with psychoanalysis.[15]

Nearly everything is said here, but differently and in a new
fashion. In the *Phenomenology of Perception,* phenomenology and
psychoanalysis were brought together by the notion that "every
human act has a meaning"—but that is not or no longer what
the later Merleau-Ponty thinks in the "Preface to Hesnard" or
in the posthumous *The Visible and the Invisible.* The philosopher
was not only always reading Freud, but also always radicalizing
the rapprochement of psychoanalysis and phenomenology in
view of their common and radical obscurity.[16] Must we still
and always leave as unquestioned or presupposed the claim
that the phenomenologist has or should have no other goal
than "leading" the pure and still mute experience "to the pure
expression of *its own meaning*"—and thus to its "signification"
or to what "makes sense" for me? In other words, is it not *too*

*much to say* that we should count on this without ceasing to believe in the possibility of the signified—especially where there is not or no longer any of it, or at least not of the kind that we would want to find? Doesn't risking a "philosophy of the limit," or developing a "limited phenomenon"[17] amount to questioning the "limits of phenomenology"?

The question of the "limit" is really posed—for Freud *to psychoanalysis* during the tragic moments of World War I and in the passing from the first to the second topography, but also *to phenomenology* in the move from the earlier (1945) to the later (1960) Merleau-Ponty. In other words, if psychoanalysis had long ago understood that a subject entirely oriented to the unveiling in consciousness (Unconscious—Preconscious—Conscious) could not suffice, phenomenology waits to draw the lesson from this. Its "coming out" or rather its "overturning" is not yet produced, which means that intentionality always remains the only requirement for its existentiality, whether in the case of the "act of consciousness" (Husserl), the "opening of Dasein" (Heidegger), the infinity of the "face" (Lévinas), the absoluteness of "givenness" (Marion), "auto-affection" (Henry), the understanding of "speech" (Chrétien) or the rupture of "liturgy" (Lacoste). To say that "all consciousness is consciousness *of* something," or that we remain with "intentionality" (German phenomenology), counter-intentionality (French phenomenology), or even the suppression of all "distance" of intentionality (Henry), is no longer sufficient today. *The "below" of sense* drills into spheres that do not reach the pair "sense" and "non-sense." Deeper and more gaping, this *stratum of the existent* says nothing and has nothing to tell me, is not seen nor is demonstrable, is not understood, and does not let itself be read. It is there, much as what Groddeck (a doctor who began a correspondence with Freud in 1917 and whose work was published in 1923) described in his *Book of the It*[18]—certainly not decipherable yet at the bottom of every act of interpretation.

Underneath the "sense of interpretation" as "the interpretation of sense" (Ricœur), there is a "backlash" of psychoanalysis on phenomenology, albeit this time disguised as a "philosophy of the Id," or of "raw nature" (Merleau-Ponty), which should now be radicalized even further in order to rid the signified definitively of any traps or presuppositions. Expecting the philosopher to see "differently" both psychoanalysis and the world as such get back neither to seeing or not seeing nor to seeing nothing, but to seeing that they see nothing precisely because there is nothing to see. To say, as I do in the title of this book, *Nothing to it*, is not to say that psychoanalysis and phenomenology neither have to collide nor to be interlaced, quite the contrary. It only shows that "to see oneself," following the Id, one first has to renounce seeing, not because one is seen *from above* in virtue of an "ego" revealed to itself, but rather because one is borne *from below* by the neuter or the "Self" of our existentiality. Latency in the Freudian sense—this hidden cache that stands in a place where there is nothing to "It"—is not "waiting" for intuition (Husserl) nor is it "withdrawn" from manifestation (Heidegger), and even less is it an excess of the invisible or the visible (Lévinas, Marion). It stands there as "different," or better, as "indifferent"—not as in agreement with another field, but in the absence of any field or horizon that would allow phenomena to appear (or not). The "Id" does not "remain," as I will show with Freud's help, rather it "resists." Something, which is not "nothing," "looks at me" and "concerns me," burying me in "hiding" according to a vulnerability one must live, rather than wanting to escape it or always trying to put it back together. Merleau-Ponty confesses in his Preface to Hesnard's *L'Œuvre de Freud*, sounding almost like an ultimatum:

> Phenomenology and psychoanalysis are not *parallel*; much better, they are both aiming toward the same *latency*. This is how I would define the relationship today, if I had to take up the questions again, not to attenuate what I said before, but, on the contrary, to make it more serious.[19]

# Go take a look

In reality, the detour through Freud and psychoanalysis has long been called for, even if "resistances" are still to be vanquished so that a philosopher comes to deal with it. From Khōra's "great bifurcation" (Derrida) to the "phenomenology of the underground" (Merleau-Ponty), the breach was already opened (*The Loving Struggle*). And the "descent into the abyss," as well as the "chaos" of our passions and our drives (*The Wedding Feast of the Lamb*), were still waiting to be analyzed *philosophically*, albeit with the help of psychoanalysis. The opening of the Hollow also implies going down into it and plumbing its depths. The plunge of the caver, like the phenomenologist in both form and in matter, can no longer be avoided. It is not sufficient merely to speak of the "abyss" or of "chaos," or "passions" or "drives." We have to do much more than that, we have to describe and go down deep into it, within the limits so remarkably laid out by Freud. The "Original Chaos" (Hesiod), the "fray of sensations" (Kant), the "world of appetites and passions" (Nietzsche), or the "region of what one can no longer say" (Heidegger), require their unfurling that a *philosophical* detour exercised by psychoanalysis is especially well situated to undertake.[1]

One can thus demand a program, but it is nothing if the piece is not played; one can declare anything, but the proclamation is worthless if it is not realized. The "Id" that has nothing to it [*n'a rien à voir*] precisely sees nothing [*ne voit rien*]. This is precisely why we, *even as philosophers*, must go to see it. Obviously we will see nothing there, at the risk of destroying with excess of visibility what still always remains hidden. Yet to see nothing is to see the nothing, or rather, it is to recognize that the *Id* that sees me requires me to see (myself) differently. "Self-knowledge" [*connaissance de soi*] is not "knowledge of myself" [*connaissance de moi*]. Yet we have to take the word literally. The Self [*Soi*] that knows me is not, or no longer only, the Ego [*Moi*] that I [*je*] know. Paradoxically, to be known by another is not, or not only, to expect everything from an alterity that would have to stare at me or would give me access to myself via the medium of my subjectivity. The other who knows me is in me—and that other is the Id [*Ça*]. "It [*Ça*] knows me," a common phrase in French suggesting a kind of connoisseurship, though this is not merely to say that I am a "connoisseur" (be it about cars or computers or philosophy) but rather it is to say quite literally that an "it" or a "neuter" within me knows me. The It/Id is not "me," not an ego or even a superego, not that by which I recognize my ego or my superego (if so one would still remain with the scheme—incessantly rehashed in both phenomenology and theology—of self-knowledge via an other), but inversely this It is the very reason that I do not know myself and will never know myself.

The "Id" does not reveal the "ego," as we have said, but rather resists it. Psychoanalysis, at least in its second topography (Id, Ego, Superego), brings the schema of transparency, or even manifestation and givenness, to an end. A necessary and irreducible obscurity is imposed in place of and instead of evidence or even of revelation. This is what psychoanalysis already knows but what phenomenology since Merleau-Ponty demands to be discovered or at least to be researched. Any phenomenologist who accepts to enter into *radical* thought, one day reaches the limits of phenomenology, and thus also of manifestation. This is not necessarily to get rid of them or leave them behind in a gesture as trivial as it is reactive, but rather to become a phenomenologist at a "higher" and "different" level—that is to say, no longer in the service of "revelation" but faced by "the crisis and the creation" (Maldiney).[2] The "It/Id" as "resistance" shares nothing with the "remainder" of a dazzling presence given in advance. "Khōra" (Derrida) or the "raw world" (Merleau-Ponty) await Freud's Id to attain the ultimate point where the "ego" or self-knowledge is no longer solely what expects to be "pacified" but also what accepts being "cornered"—in self-struggle within the Self, because that place is also where the highest level of creativity lies.[3]

# CHAPTER ONE

# Keep moving, nothing to see

"Keep moving, there is nothing to see": this phrase is well known—used both as a leitmotif for law enforcement agencies on the roads and also for what should be an inquiry into the limits of phenomenality. Perhaps *we see too much*, if not in psychoanalysis, then at least in phenomenology. Almost at the very beginning of his Preface to Hesnard's *L'Œuvre de Freud*, Merleau-Ponty warns within a few lines of each other, putting "both" phenomenology "and" psychoanalysis on the lookout: "*Phenomenological idealism* is insufficient," and "there is an *idealist deviation of Freudian research* alongside the objectivist deviation."[1] Just before his death, Merleau-Ponty sees or understands that idealism has invaded everything, without resolving its mystery but by setting the terms for it. From the side of phenomenology, the reduction to the lived experience of consciousness lacks bodily incarnation, at least in the early Husserl (in the 1913 *Ideas I*), from the other side, the scientific claim of psychoanalysis still takes the psyche as a system in the early Freud (in the 1910 *Five Lessons on Psychoanalysis*). In short, everything is constructed or constructs itself "from the noetic-noematic correlation" in Husserl or, in Freud, passes through the "censor" of the orderly agency of the preconscious situated between the conscious and the unconscious. The ideals of the Enlightenment and of the progress of knowledge inhabit Husserl the mathematician as much as Freud the doctor in the period prior to the war. To know oneself by oneself, including one's psyche, is also in some way to objectify oneself. As a proof, consider Freud's declaration to an audience of young psychoanalysts during the 1910 Nuremberg Congress at the end of a paper on "Future Prospects of Psycho-Analysis":

> you are not only giving your patients the most efficacious remedy for their sufferings that is available to-day; you are contributing your share to the Enlightenment [*Aufklärung*] of the community from which we expect to achieve the most radical prophylaxis against neurotic disorders along the indirect path of social authority.[2]

## *The end of the Enlightenment*

So what has happened for psychoanalysis and Freud himself to have changed so much—from the stated Enlightenment ideal on which the first topography that is entirely oriented toward consciousness still depends (1895-1914)—to the plunge into obscurity and the Id's resistance in the second topography (1914-1939)? First and foremost, the War (July 1914) and the first awareness that this drama is "for culture as well," as we see both in Freud's correspondence with Lou Andreas-Salomé and in the text titled *Thoughts for the Times on War and Death* (November 1914). Then the death of his daughter Sophie, the mother of little Ernst, to which the work *Beyond the Pleasure Principle* will bear witness regardless of what its author says (1920). Finally, the announcement of his jaw cancer, which is exactly contemporaneous with *The Ego and the Id* (1923). The conclusion of *Moses and Monotheism* (1938) on the eve of his death (1939)—and on this point one could not be clearer— radically distances his thought from the Enlightenment ideal and from the Enlightenment sense of progress announced in 1910: "We are living in a specially remarkable period. We find to our astonishment that progress has *allied itself with barbarism.*"[3]

But is it enough to notice the catastrophe to provide commentary on it or, indeed, to understand it? What can the incessant and impressive *Freudian deepening*, always in search of the truth about the self, still teach the philosopher today about his or her own quest for phenomenality without leaving him or her, even existentially, only in the presupposition of the "sensed"? Better still, must not the very idea that "*there is meaning*" be questioned? In reality, it all depends on the value *gnothi seauton* or "self-knowledge" has "for today." Knowing oneself after Freud or Merleau-Ponty certainly comes down to knowing that one cannot know oneself. Yet in this case not because we would be unknowable to ourselves in the sense of an unfathomable mystery (negative theology) or because we would need another to be known (recourse to transcendence), but in my view just because the "Self" resists the "Ego" that wants to know it, thus questioning the very model of knowledge and requiring maybe not its rejection but at least its modification. Perhaps the "self" to be "known" is never "known" except through the "attack" or the "backlash" of psychoanalysis on phenomenology, thus through the disqualification of the mode of access (knowledge) by which we always try to reach and delimit it. Keep moving, "there is nothing to see" does not simply mean that we see too much, according to the shared ideal of the beginnings of psychoanalysis and phenomenology now to be overcome, but rather that *seeing* is not or is no longer adapted to thinking. That there is "nothing to see" and that we therefore must "keep moving" and not "linger" at a scene made for gapers who have no business there and who are incapable of being bothered by a spectacle that never actually disrupts them—such is the first and great turn that Merleau-Ponty—in this regard Freud's heir—imposed on phenomenology. Self-knowledge must be "ontologized" in order to be thought—not only to presuppose that we are or even can be known, but to question the *being* that knows, in its capacities as well as in its impossibilities: the "knowing as such."

## Toward another paradigm

By way of Freud, then, but according to a movement that will only progressively be specified, the passage from "seeing" to "touching," and then to the "touching touched" in Merleau-Ponty comes precisely from this same necessity of furnishing a new paradigm of knowledge. Indeed, any history of philosophy has really always been based on a model of "seeing": from its birth (*idein* as seeing in Plato or the *sight* that gives humans the natural desire to know in Aristotle), to its deployment (*intuition* or *intuere* as seeing in Descartes) to its completion (*the Absolute* in Hegel) and its supposed overcoming (the *clearing* of Being in

Heidegger). One may have wanted to overcome metaphysics, but one nevertheless remained within the model of metaphysics (even in Heidegger): a model of vision, intuition, unveiling, and thus of manifestation. In this regard, the change in paradigm initiated by Merleau-Ponty is radical, even though we have not yet drawn all the lessons from it. Moving from "seeing" to "touching," the author of the *Phenomenology of Perception* is not simply going from one "sense" (sight) to an "other" (touch) but is calling into question the very mode of thinking—as with Lévinas later, marshalling the "caress" against "vision" in *Totality and Infinity*.[4]

The two reasons for the requalification of "touching" relative to "seeing" in Merleau-Ponty are well known. I will recall them here not to develop them but in order to draw out their consequences, at least for the radicalization of thought. First, the touching-touched of myself, "when my left hand touches my right hand and vice versa" calls into question the dissociation of subject and object, since I no longer know which "is the hand which is touching" and which "is the hand being touched."[5] Secondly, the "touching touched" of the other allows me to attain a sort of "happy obscurity," in line with what we ordinarily call the "mystery of the fourth term." For if "I sense" others when I shake their hand or when I caress them, "I sense that I am sensed" (I re-sense), "I sense that the other senses" (the clash or product of enjoyment), but I do not sense "*what* they sense." The impossibility of feeling what the other feels, even though I feel, even though I sense that I sense and sense that the other senses, precisely opens onto what I have elsewhere called the "vulnerabilities of the flesh,"[6] in that the impossibility of sensing or feeling others imposes the recourse to speech in order for them to tell me what they feel. Speech complements or completes the flesh, certainly in eros but perhaps also in the psychoanalytic situation between doctor and patient, wherein the failure in re-sensing the other's feeling requires the other to speak in order to express it. The obscurity is not regrettable; quite the contrary: It is "blessed" in that it does not have to be unveiled (perhaps it has to leave behind the ideal of transparency or the illusion of the manifest), but instead has to be said through a body of speech that alone is capable of incarnating it or at least of expressing it.[7] In short, the end of the primacy of seeing over touching requires us, at least in phenomenology, to *think otherwise*: to think beyond the strict dissociation of subject and object (whence the Merleau-Pontian chiasm), and beyond the ideal of the transparency of manifesting and knowing everything (whence the critique, also Merleau-Pontian, of that transcendence coming from above).

## *Collapse of the system*

Accordingly and paradoxically, what is produced in phenomenology is expressed similarly in psychoanalysis. For in reading carefully Freud's first great theoretical description of the first topography in *Metapsychology* (1915), we easily see that the system of three well-differentiated, separated, sealed-off and orderly agencies no longer holds up, and already begins to disintegrate. Indeed, starting in his synthetic text called *The Unconscious* (1915), psychoanalysis (which Freud calls a "depth psychology") makes the "censor" between the unconscious and the conscious intervene like "a sort of trial." There would thus be *three* rather than *two* agencies in the first topography. But from the start, the founder of psychoanalysis neither seem to want nor be able to separate easily what an overly-"oiled" systematic could try to dissociate or even to simplify: "By accepting the existence of these [*two or three*] psychical systems, psychoanalysis has departed a step further from the descriptive 'psychology of consciousness'."[8] Better—and here the drama starts to emerge or the Enlightenment-era theoretical construction to thicken—Freud admits: "I am of the opinion that the antithesis of conscious and unconscious *is not applicable* to instincts."[9] The entire first topography, which was originally oriented to consciousness and as such was based on the "model of seeing" (even though the process of the drive, of repression or sublimation tended to be either opposed to it or to disguise it), already begins to turn back on itself or to shake in its very foundations. Not inasmuch as "seeing" would be "being seen," but rather in that "*there is nothing to see,*" because, as Merleau-Ponty will denounce later on, all metaphysical thought wants only "to see" and "to see everything," on the basis of the mere fact alone that it "is seen" and "sees itself seeing."

As Freud once again confesses, this time calling philosophy itself into question: "The more we seek to win our way to a metapsychological view of mental life, the more we must learn to emancipate ourselves from the importance of *the symptom of 'being conscious.'* So long as we still cling to this belief we see our generalizations regularly broken through by exceptions."[10] The exception—what escapes from the symptom of "being conscious"—thus becomes the rule. Or rather the rule—the general orientation toward consciousness—does not resist or no longer resists the exception. One can certainly conceive of three agencies of one well-ordered topography and thus claim a sort of scientificity; analysis and experience disqualify the subsequently-denounced "ego ideal." The "Self" [*Soi*] in Nietzsche, like the "Id" [*Ça*] in Freud, as we shall see later, submits the "Ego" [*Moi*] or subjectivity to trial by catastrophe, such that the "I" [*Je*] can be affirmed only in a struggle where it would falsely come to break away. The "topological" (or geographical, to use Freud's word) point of view of the psyche in the division of agencies progressively cedes its place to the "economic" (quantity of energy) and "dynamic" (conflict of the drives) point of view. In the eyes of the Viennese psychoanalyst, what happens between the "States"—the barbarism of the first months of World War I—also affects the ego. Freud recognizes in *Thoughts for the Times on War and Death* that: "We cannot but feel that no event has ever destroyed so much that is precious in the common possessions of humanity, *confused so many* of the clearest *intelligences*, or so thoroughly *debased* what is highest."[11]

The First World War is thus for Freud, the founder of psychoanalysis, not only a "crisis," as it will be later for Husserl, the founder of phenomenology (in the 1936 *Crisis of the European Sciences and of Transcendental Phenomenology*). It is properly speaking a "revolution," the imposition of a change of paradigm and not merely the correction of an old system. As Freud avers just six months after the declaration of a war that already saw 360,000 French soldiers killed (60,000 per month on average, and more than a million when we include all the parties involved in the fighting): "*We refused to believe it*; but *how would we picture* such a war if we had to do so?"[12]

In the still nascent eyes of psychoanalysis, the Great War is not simply political or military. It is *metaphysical*. It introduces the *unrepresentable* into the heart of the ego and destroys not only the ego's capacity to present or to be represented, but the very idea that there is something to "present" or something "representable." The First World War for Freud, like the Second World War and the question of "evil" for the phenomenology of Emmanuel Lévinas,[13] was not produced in a horizon—it suppresses *in ovo* the very capacity to open a horizon. There is schizophrenia or separation in the war because there is separation or schizophrenia in the ego. Such is Freud's discovery, who, contrary to his philosophical contemporaries (Husserl, Bergson, Russell), will "*beware of it*"—in all senses of the term: the "it" of the event of the war and the "it/id" of the submission or even of the annihilation of the ego.

# Chapter Two

# Beware of it

To say *Nothing to It*, as in the title of the present essay, is no longer and not simply to criticize the idealist deviations in phenomenology and psychoanalysis, nor is it to give up on the "seeing" that makes inaccessible an It that one could possibly "touch" (in a feedback from Merleau-Ponty to Freud), but rather to agree now to *beware of "It"*—that is, to bring our attention to bear on our own barbarism, there where one would neither be able to believe it nor be able to be convinced of it. Alone—that is, without the disparagement or pan-Germanism that inhabits any number of his contemporaries (Husserl in particular)[1]—Freud takes account of trauma in the spectacle of the war unfolding before his eyes—and on this subject he engages in a long and fruitful correspondence with Lou Andreas-Salomé. On November 19th, 1914, Andreas-Salomé, who was friend and confidante to both Nietzsche and Rilke, confides to Freud that:

Every day one is confronted by the same task: to try and *conceive the inconceivable*. One works one's way through this cruelly destructive time as through a thickset thorn bush. I cannot think of any personal fate which could have cost me anything like such anguish. And I don't really believe *that after this* we shall ever be able *to be really happy again*.[2]

## Conceiving the inconceivable

"Conceiving the inconceivable"—this is the path to take if one wants to *beware of "it"* or even *beware of the "Id."* For what happens during the First World War is not an "ideology" but rather "barbarism"—and this is in truth what separates the two great wars of the twentieth century from each other. One knows why people die, or rather why there is death in the Second World War, because it is thoroughly "rationalized" even if it is never "reasonable." Although one may die for nothing, it is all the same under a strongly asserted *ideology*, program, or cause (Nazism). Inversely, one does not die merely for nothing during the First World War, but one does not know *why* one dies, who dies, or where the people who die go or might want to go. The military blocks confront one another in a quasi-irrational way, and *barbarism* is the blindness of a violence devoid of all meaning, as with any ideology. As Freud, both clairvoyant and disappointed, claims:

Then the war in which we had refused to believe broke out, and it brought—*disillusionment*.... It *tramples* in "blind fury" on all that comes in its way, as though there were to be no future and no peace among men after it is over.... Indeed, one of the great civilized nations [France] is so universally unpopular that the attempt can actually be made to exclude it from the civilized community as 'barbaric,' although it has long proved its fitness by the magnificent contributions to that community which it has made.[3]

Despite their great lucidity, these statements would not really help us if they did not lead us a step further into the dizzying descent into our humanity. Freud's response to Lou Andreas-Salomé is maybe not proof, but at least a sign of it. The question in this war is not simply about military conflict, but also about *psychoanalysis* itself. Neither insofar as psychoanalysis aims to declare war on the war, nor that it would itself be a war, but rather to the extent that the "barbarism" in question was always what psychoanalysis had been reaching for. It was what psychoanalysis had to say, what it had to think from the moment of its birth—but what it had not yet reached, said, or thought. Or, rather, it had reached, said and thought it, but without having really felt or experienced it. Freud writes a few days later (on 25 November 1914) in response to his confidante: "I do not doubt that humanity will survive even this war, but I know for certain that for me and my contemporaries the world will never again be a happy place. It is too hideous. And the *saddest* thing about it is that it is exactly *the way we should have expected people to behave* from our *knowledge of psychoanalysis*."[4]

The "saddest" thing about the war, then—if we can claim this following Freud—is not simply the millions of deaths in just a few months, nor the hatred of peoples, nor the incomprehensibility of the tragedy of death, but that *psychoanalysis itself* had not yet known or been able to reach its goal.

## *The disillusion of psychoanalysis*

The "disillusionment caused by the war" and the "attitude toward death" that make up the two parts of the *Thoughts for the Times on War and Death* (1915) can thus be read as the "disillusionment of psychoanalysis itself" on the one hand, and as the first discovery of the "death drive" on the other. For what is true in war and for those "over there" on the front is also at least as true for those who are "here" as observers of this disaster—those whom Freud called "those who stayed home" (or the "rearguard") to whom he belongs, while undertaking his own battle to get to the bottom of the Self:

> We must restrict ourselves to the second group, to which we ourselves belong. I have said already that in my opinion the bewilderment and the paralysis of our capacity of implementation, from which we suffer, are essentially determined among other things by the circumstance that *we are unable to maintain our former attitude towards death,* and have *not yet found a new one.*[5]

The political war of the military units between the peoples (political and military aims) accordingly also refers to the internal conflict of the passions and drives in the self (psychoanalysis). Thus, if the war led to "disillusionment" (because we would never have believed that people could be capable of such "barbarism"), so too will psychoanalytical therapy be disillusioned, and hence will have to change, or at least deepen, its orientation. With the Great War, the ideal of the Enlightenment or the enlightenment ideal of psychoanalysis, as well as the orientation of the libidinal drives toward consciousness, as articulated in the first topography, suffer their first knockout blow:

> Students of human nature and philosophers have long taught us that *we are mistaken* in regarding our intelligence as an independent force and in overlooking its *dependence on emotional life.* ... the *man of prehistoric times* survives *unchanged* in our unconscious.[6]

## Primitive man

From war and the primitive drives that are awakened in armies, we learn that we have never fallen "from on high" because our civilization was in reality always already "down low," it just did not know this. It would be too simplistic to believe that barbarism made us fall from the civilized, or that we were once "angels" who have now become "beasts." In reality, we have always been (from the) "beasts," but we did not want to believe it and had not seen ourselves as such. Only war will show it in peoples—and it is equally the task of psychoanalysis, or today even of phenomenology, to show it in individuals: "… our fellow citizens *have not sunk so low* as we feared, because they had never *risen so high* as we believed."[7] The war and its unpunished murders, site of the absolute freedom of the passions and drives, bring forth the "naked," or even "raw," unconscious. The "death drive" now concerns *us* and reaches *us*—not only via the millions of soldiers who fell at the front, but also via any human "ego," including first and foremost the founder of psychoanalysis, suddenly stripped of all his illusions ever truly to reach or know the self. The awareness that had once been taken as a symptom and thus by way of a decorous and sublimated manifestation of the passions had only covered over what we truly are, at least a part of which the death drive will progressively exhibit, and so, "if we are to be judged by our unconscious wishful impulses, *we ourselves are, like primeval man, a gang of murderers.*"[8]

Probably only one person—Franz Rosenzweig—knew this, precisely because he was at the front, drafting on postcards in the trenches in the Balkans in 1917 what would later become *The Star of Redemption*, published for the first time in 1921 when it went largely unnoticed. Groddeck's *The Book of the It* had not yet been published (1923), but, as mentioned before, a correspondence with Freud nevertheless bears witness to similar research in this same war year (1917). The philosopher Rosenzweig opens *The Star of Redemption* with a rarely equaled tragic account of death—one that the violence of combat will exacerbate or at least lend support to what will bring to a close the irenics of the *Enlightenment* (that one had now been proven wrong to share). As one reads in the opening sentence or *princeps* of this work: "It is from death, from the fear of death, that any knowledge of the Whole begins. *Philosophy has the audacity* to cast off the fear of the earthly, to remove from death its poisonous sting, from Hades its pestilential breath."[9]

The "displaced" or "disconnected" character of any philosophy tending to close itself up in totality ends with Rosenzweig and the horror of death in the trenches. Similarly with Freud, and with regard to the same war, one enters into a radical "disillusionment of psychoanalysis," which committed the error or the audacity to want to explain everything.

Yet more, and something better, appears in the relation of Rosenzweig to Freud or even in relation to Groddeck or to Nietzsche. For even in, or maybe first of all in, Rosenzweig, the "Id/It" (*das Es*) specifically emerges over against the "ego" or directs the "ego" (*das Ich*), turning the *reality* of death rather than its mere possibility (Heidegger), into the privileged source of the most complete destructiveness. For not only "subjects" or even "individuals" die in World War I, but beings and people whose annihilation is such that "egoity" (the I) is reduced to pure and simple neutrality ("it"), before rebelling in order to recover an identity. Because one no longer knows *who* dies when one dies at the front—and in the violence of "shredded flesh" or "cannon fodder"—the word "Id/It" (*das Es*) erupts in the course of a sentence at the very opening of *The Star of Redemption*: "*sein Ich nur ein Es wäre* (his *I* would be only an *it*)." When in its blindness violence reaches its most extreme point, absolute evil or the "unpitiable" no longer lets itself be "seen" or even "suffered," at least inasmuch as the "I" becomes suddenly and radically reduced to the "it" or, in other words, identity is reduced to anonymity beyond any alterity. As the philosopher of the "trenches" writes in a gripping fashion:

> That man may crawl like a worm into the folds of the naked earth before whizzing projectiles of blind pitiless death, or that there he may feel as violently inevitable that which he never feels otherwise: his *I* would be only an *It* [*sein Ich nur ein Es wäre*] if it were to die; and he may cry out his I with every cry still in his throat against the Pitiless One by whom he is threatened with such an unimaginable annihilation.[10]

As I have said, Freud's *disillusionment in psychoanalysis* finds its successor, or rather its counterpart, in Rosenzweig's *disillusionment with philosophy*. Philosophers or theologians have wrongly made us believe in the beyond, or at least in its easy access, although according to the Jewish philosopher there is no Revelation except via " the possibility of experiencing a miracle."[11] The onset or imminence of death inevitably maintains the existent in reality or in attachment to the here and now. The "desire for death" or any escape into a netherworld cannot hide the insuppressible "desire to live" in the proximity of death—whether it be in the trenches where one always prefers to remain alive rather than to die, even in danger of suffocation, or in psychoanalysis, where—as we shall see—the "death drive" (the return to the inorganic) is always counterbalanced by a "life drive" (sexuality).

The philosopher of *The Star of Redemption* concludes his essay much in the way that Freud concludes the *Thoughts for the Times on War and Death*:

> Upon all this misery, philosophy smiles its empty smile and, with its outstretched index finger, shows

the creature, whose limbs are trembling in fear for
its life in this world, a world beyond, of which it
wants to know nothing at all. For man does not
at all want to escape some chain; he wants to stay,
he wants—to live (*er will bleiben, er will—leben*).
… Man feels only too well that he is certainly
condemned to death, but not to suicide.[12]

Freud and Rosenzweig's contemporaneity with the Great
War is noteworthy here—but one of them is "a soldier on the
front lines" in the trenches and subject to death in a nearly
unheard-of fashion, while the other is "in the rear guard," safely
ensconced in his psychoanalytic consulting rooms, keeping silent
in the face of such brutality that demands a different kind of
thinking. All the same, one finds neither flight nor laziness in the
psychoanalyst in his refuge in Vienna—but rather an eminent
courage of thought. For after Freud, everything has to start over.
Turning meaning "upside down," abandoning the cosmos to
descend into chaos, agreeing to sink below rather than always
wanting to climb up. *Primitive man* arises in an exemplary
fashion, and a war—yet what kind of war! —is enough for the
"Id" to begin to emerge, or rather to resist.

There had been "humanity" taken up in the "ego," and a
part of animality made up of passions and drives had already
been discovered in us. With "animality," we then also found
the potentiality of "bestiality" as a kind of supplement, albeit
as fall toward a possible below animality (*Wedding Feast of the
Lamb*). But with the Id, there now arises evidence that there
is something worse than "bestiality," namely, *its* real power in
"brutality" (*nothing to It*). "*Becoming brute*"—to borrow a phrase
from Henri de Lubac commenting on Pico della Mirandola—

names the way that the human here touches "the lowest" (not mere sin but the reduction to nothingness or acedia), and that the divine will endeavor to transform in order to raise it to "the highest" (by the redemption of all or *anakephalaiosis*): "To animalization and, if we dare say, to the '*becoming brute*' of the sinner, responds, in contrast, the transformation or the transfiguration of the elected in God."[13]

That there is an "Id" prior to an "Ego" (Freud) or a "Self" prior to the "me" (Nietzsche) is the lesson drawn from the conflict—not primarily military or political, but metaphysical—from which Freud and we after him have not finished drawing the lessons for philosophy itself.[14] For the least one can say is that every "Id" *is not nothing*, inasmuch as the Id subsists first as an insuppressible resistance rooted in the "organic" and insofar as missing the corporeal would mean to flee the reality of the instinctual. Withdrawing into and preferring the Symbolic to the organic or advocating the linguistic in order to influence the somatic, is what *the father of psychoanalysis* would never want or do, because the drive "at the frontier of the psychic and the somatic" will never totally leave the earth from which it arose.

CHAPTER THREE

# It's not nothing

Freud therefore does not stop there. The forward march continues, not only the march of the "red pants" to the front,[1] but rather the march into the equally war-like terrain of psychoanalysis itself, the terrain of the Id's "resistance" and of the discovery of another and new "front" that takes hold in me. And in all of that, as we have said, "'it is not nothing." This is not simply a matter of playing with words or a ludic paraphrase devoid of meaning around an "It" by way of a totem that would lead the dance.

*Nothing to It*, the title of this essay, certainly requires to "keep moving because there is nothing to see" (idealization and disqualification of the model of seeing), and to *beware of It* (disillusionment and death as the two traits, not merely of war but also of psychoanalysis itself). But it is still necessary to recognize that *It is not nothing*—not solely insofar as the Id is something, but rather because this marks the gravity of the thing. "It's not nothing" in the common sense of the term: because the event of the war and the subsequent calling into question (the move from the first to the second topography) launches a challenge to psychoanalysis that will make it at least budge if not change. In short, one "has to do it"—not only thinking through the war, but thinking oneself thinking through the war, and showing that the *thought of the war* becomes precisely the place of and the tool for the destruction of all thought. In fact, it is simply not enough to discover the "drive" or even to glimpse its savagery, as soon as the event of war has taught us that "primitive man survives as such in our unconscious." One must now talk about the "instinctual," and even root it in itself, or rather, in the Self, if one indeed wants to set out on the impossible quest or even conquest of the ego. The "somatic," or even the "organic," comes in here, which is precisely *not nothing* insofar as it exacerbates the Id, gives it weight, and definitively anchors it in infra-linguistic corporeality, which at least in Freud does not pass through the "collective" (Jung) or the "symbolic" (Lacan).

### The drive at the frontier

Starting in 1915, after preparing and editing the text of the *Thoughts for the Times on War and Death*, at the same time as the correspondence with Lou Andreas-Salomé (the end of 1914), Freud is working on his new essay on *Drives and their Vicissitudes* (1915), its aspiration being, as we know, not only to define force but also and above all to align it with the body. At the beginning of this work, we read the famous definition: "the concept of 'drive' appears to us as *a limit-concept between the mental and the somatic*."[2]

We will not here rehearse the long Freudian analysis distinguishing the "drive" on the one hand from "instinct" (which is always hereditary and preformed as in the animal) and on the other from "excitation" (which is only physiological and belongs to the order of the reflex)—but we will note that the analysis pursues a single goal: to show that *the human alone is capable of drives*, much as Heidegger will later say that "Dasein (alone) exists."[3] For the drive (*Trieb*) is neither exclusively psychic nor merely somatic, but on the border between the two. The drive as a "limit-concept," strictly speaking, is not an extreme concept (like the "limit situation" in Jaspers),[4] but rather it is a concept that takes on the limit, inhabits the limit, or camps out on its frontier. In 1915, prior to the introduction of the death drive despite having already perceived the ambivalence of love and hatred, the drive includes only the "drive for self-preservation" (the ego drive) and the sexual drive (later also understood as a life drive). As Freud indicates at the time, it is known only by its "goal" (its satisfaction), or by its object (its hold), but never in its drive as such (its "morsel of activity") nor in its source (its "somatic process"). What matters here on the route toward the Id that we are retracing with Freud is less the drive itself than its mode of knowing: "Known as unknown," to borrow a phrase from negative theology.

Yet we must be clear here. The drive, my drive—the force in me that I do not always recognize as being me—appears to me as "a known that is unknown." But this does not mean that it exceeds me like the divine (the path from above); rather it descends into and inhabits the depths of the human (the path from below). What determines the drive (at least in this period) is not merely the psychic but rather and primarily the somatic: "drives are wholly determined *by their origin in a somatic source*."[5]

Freud will surely evolve in the determination of the drive, which will become more psychic than somatic with the irruption of the death drive in *Beyond the Pleasure Principle* (1920). Yet the main task is done and something good (rather than evil) has come out of it. If it is not rooted in the body, the drive loses both its carnal consistency and its foundation in the Id. By distinguishing the drive from instinct or excitation, Freud does not aim to disincarnate it, although that is sometimes wrongly thought. The drive instead wants to be rooted in the "human" body and exists only insofar as it is nourished *at the same time* by the psychic and the somatic, maintaining itself "on the border" or "at the limit" of their crossing and cohabitation. What concerns the drive is not solely psychic but also organic—their link or nexus constitutes the drive as such.

### Rooting in the organic

To confront psychoanalysis with phenomenology while recognizing the importance that Husserl or Merleau-Ponty grant to the "flesh" (*Leib*) and to the "body" (*Körper*), a philosopher may rightly regret that subsequent psychoanalysis, and in particular in the Lacanian interpretation of the Freudian drives, omits the "somatic" from the drive in order to interpret it only in a "symbolic" or "linguistic" manner. As Lacan insists in Seminar II with respect to the drive in Freud: "What I teach you about Freud. . . is that we have no means of apprehending *this* real—on any level and not only on that of knowledge—except via the go-between of the *symbolic*."[6]

I agree with Rudolf Bernet here who says that "evoking only very briefly the 'source' of drive-based life, Lacan remains silent on the *somatic origin* of the drive."[7] The (somatic) point of departure for the drive is forgotten, and this is why it becomes gradually disincarnated. In an effort to humanize it, even to center experience on its linguistic mode, we progressively lose what comes from the weight of our animality, even our bestiality, our own organicity, and even our brutality. This is what the Freudian beginning had not omitted in regard to the drive, and so we must go back to it in order not to neglect an Id that traces out the contours of a humanity defined not by its linguistic context, but rather by its bodily weight, without which it would not be able to exist.

The *backlash* of psychoanalysis on phenomenology certainly goes in at least one direction, namely, the obscure point of what is below or beneath any signification intended by the Freudian "unconscious" and recovered in the Merleau-Pontyan "raw nature" or the Derridean *Khōra*. But it also leads in another direction, namely the necessity for psychoanalysis itself not to lose its corporeal rootedness—which constitutes phenomenology's strongest point. At the very point where the disciplines would falsely claim their autonomy or their impermeability, in fact, their intersection makes newly visible how their encounter leads to deepening the path of each without ever competing against each other. Psychoanalysis leads phenomenology back to its *Urgrund* or toward the "obscure ground" of the human, which it cannot avoid, and, conversely, phenomenology demands of psychoanalysis not to forget the "incarnated" and thus the corporeity from which it initially developed.

"*It*, therefore, is not nothing"—although that does not turn it into a "something" that might as well reify it. What the Id or at least its inner drive teaches us is first and essentially to come back to the organic body and not be satisfied with any attempted escape from it into the psychic. It bears the weight of "suffering" or rather always anchors the psychic to the somatic in such a way that the drive lives on the border, or better, *is* the border itself. We must go down into our own chaos made up of these drives and passions with the help of either a psychology or a phenomenology of "the depths," in order to recover the power of the "force" that constitutes us, instead of always being satisfied with the (certainly necessary but not sufficient) standards of passivity and alterity that make us forget what there is of the "will" and its own power.

We have elsewhere said that contemporary phenomenology suffers from a triple hypertrophy—of the "flesh" over the "body" (for which Merleau-Ponty is not the least responsible), of "meaning" over "chaos" (since the first determination of intentionality in Husserl), and of "passivity" over "activity" or of "weakness" over "force" (according to the false interpretations of the welcome of the other or the face in Lévinas, for example).[8] The Freudian drive—rooted in a *body* that is not only *flesh* (return to the organic), *chaotic* or swirling in the magma of the Id beneath all givenness or orientation of the drive (like Nietzsche in this second topography), and in collusion with *force* rather than with passivity (for which Spinoza is the prime origin)—thus imposes on the phenomenologist the task of thinking *otherwise or differently*, and thus of revisiting his standards linked to the always already presupposed signifieds.

## Presence and resistance

*It is not nothing*, and thus the drive itself is defined as "the" something at the origin of everything. That means that the ego is nourished and is progressively discovered to be inhabited by the stranger within it, which makes it wonder by way of a final reminder: "*What is It?*" Make no mistake. This formulation would neither want to "define" the drive nor enclose in its *quid* what would not belong to it. For the Id precisely has no limits, inasmuch as it is the Unlimited and produces limits. The Id is neither contained in a signifier nor designates a signified, but rather questions the very possibility of the act of "signifying" and thus of a horizon that would still hold onto the "sensible." Without deciding for or against "sense" or "non-sense," the Id remains *beneath* the very question of sense, and thus of the given. One can wonder "what gives," but one must still define or presuppose something to be given, or at least handed out. The *privative* of signification (in the expectation of what should "give" or "signify") does not reach the *negative* of signification (in an "extra-phenomenal" that is incapable of presupposing it).

The "*what is It?*" thus does not say that the "Id" is "some thing" or "a something" or even any "thing," as we have said, but rather it deploys the necessity or existence of a Neuter or of a resistance to thought—which psychoanalysis in its quest for the drive tried to analyze and which phenomenology is today succeeding in finding again. Surely, we will not say that the drive or *Trieb* has never been philosophically analyzed in the originary framework of the unfolding of phenomenality (Husserl), but its treatment does not share anything with what psychoanalysis never stopped looking for. The Freudian drive is at antipodes with the Husserlian drive, inasmuch as the former reaches the magma of a Neuter or of an Id originally capable of constituting us, while the latter questions the "layers of the signified" in the so-called "impressional sphere," not to call intentionality into question but on the contrary to ground it.[9] In short, the "drive" [*Trieb*] is not the same because the aim is inverted: the bedrock of the unconscious on the one hand, and the presupposition of the signified on the other. In his chapter "Force and Signification," Jacques Derrida writes: "Now, one would seek in vain a concept in phenomenology which would permit the conceptualization of *intensity* or *force*. The conceptualization not only of *direction* but of *power*, not only the *in* but the *tension* of intentionality."[10]

The "backlash" of psychoanalysis on phenomenology thus does not require first *phenomenologically* deploying what psychoanalysis had already *psychologically* treated, which is always just a way of appropriating the field of the other, but rather acknowledging that one can oneself be "modified" by what the other had unfolded. If the "direction" has taken place and introduced "tension" into phenomenology (according to a judgment to which we could add nuance on the basis of Husserl's unpublished manuscripts),[11] or if a forgetfulness of "force" has to be recognized at the expense of "signification," this in no way indicates that one must necessarily *leave* phenomenology behind. The Derridean judgment that "emancipation from this (phenomenological) language must be attempted"[12] is probably too severe or even useless. One does not gather the "crops from a field" by abandoning it, but by working on it in a different manner. All the same, the Freudian Id calls into question intentionality and its determination always to signify. Merleau-Ponty had himself opened the way, less to extricate himself from phenomenology than to inhabit it anew, less to combat it than to orient it in a different way: "What *resists* phenomenology *in us*—naturally being, the 'barbaric principle' of which Schelling spoke—*cannot remain outside of phenomenology* and *must find its place within it.*"[13]

The *"What is It?"* [or, more idiomatically, "What is that exactly?"] thus questions the nature of the agency here designated, whose content, as we have shown, refers first of all to the instinctual, and even to corporeity. Yet, the common French expression: *what is it?* also makes reference to the strange, even to the "thingamajig" of a being or an object so unfamiliar that it becomes impossible to name it. "*What's that?*": it is something that is not nothing, but about which we cannot definitively say "what it is," or even "what use it has." To remain at the border, on the frontier, of what can be said as soon as we reach the limit or the "extra-phenomenal"—such are the stakes of a discourse that does not flee into the insignificant, but says, at least in a negative way, what there is of the chasm of the human—we must descend into the "depth" or "underground" of this chasm rather than seeking to fill it up.

Chapter Four

# What is it?

*A disturbing uncanny*

While going from *Drives and their Vicissitudes* (1915) to *Beyond the Pleasure Principle* (1920), the war has come to an end, assuming something of this sort were possible. Thus, the world finds itself and lives in what Freud in 1919 calls a "feeling of the uncanny," a "disturbing strangeness" [*inquiétante étrangeté*] in the sense of the "familiar" having become "uncanny and frightening."[1] What "disturbs" is not that the world has changed, but rather, that we who are in the world have changed. It is as if the ego [*le moi*] were not me [*moi*], or rather no longer me [*moi*]. Freud indicates specifically that:

> This uncanny (*Dieses Unheimliche*) is in reality nothing new or alien, but something which is

familiar and old-established in the mind and which has become alienated from it only through the process of repression.[2]

The uncanny, this *disturbing strangeness*, he adds, would thus be "something which ought to have remained hidden but has come to light."[3] With the aid of Schelling's *Urgrund* and of evil's irruption from this "originary ground" cited specifically by Freud, what is forbidden thus seems to be transgressed, the hidden becomes manifest, and the obscure comes out from the shadows.

Yet is there something really given to see here? Nothing is less certain. For in the battle of the drives, whether it concerns "war" or "repetition," the *natural character* of death is always on the horizon. Death "always marks the end of life" insofar as it is inherent in every living creature, constituting it as such, and never occurs to it by simple accident: "all living substance is bound to die from internal causes."[4] However debatable such a definition may be (death by programmed degeneration nevertheless demonstrated today by the biological mechanism of apoptosis), what matters for Freud is first what it engenders for the point of view of thought: the Id as a sort of magma toward which to return.

### Death and repetition

We know that the tragic event of the death of Sophie, Freud's daughter and the mother of his grandson Ernst, hero of the *Fort-Da*, marks the writing of *Beyond the Pleasure Principle*— even against the author's will. The note making allusion to this in the text is striking, signaling at once both distance (because the doctor always wants to maintain objectivity), and proximity (inasmuch as his exaggerated modesty could not be camouflaged here):

> When this child was five and three-quarters [the little Ernst who had been one and a half when playing with the reel], *his mother died* [without naming Sophie or mentioning Freud's own paternity]. Now that she was really 'gone' (o-o-o), the little boy showed no signs of grief (*Trauer*). It is true that *in the interval a second child had been born* and had roused him to violent jealousy.[5]

Death is there, which not only "comes to the door and knocks," but which has "already knocked," in every sense of the term, in such a way that its sickle had come to decimate nearly everything within the Freud family—at the very least distraught at having been affected this much, even when these events would remain within the sphere of the private.

Everything is thus an "affair of death" in this beyond—which might actually be a "below"—of the pleasure principle.[6] A single logic governs both the memory of the trauma of the war (soldiers returning from the front) and the *Fort-Da* game of little Ernst. In the two cases, in the form of examples that follow the opening to *Beyond the Pleasure Principle*, "death" or "absence" guides the symbolic game of repetition as if in a sort of "compulsion." The traumatizing images of the war never stop arising [*survenir*] and returning [*revenir*] to the memory of those who were engaged in it. One thus has to "deal with death," not because it has come, but because one has survived it.

As Freud already indicated in his *Introduction to Psycho-Analysis and the War Neuroses* (1919): "… in the case of war neuroses, in contrast to the pure traumatic neuroses… what is feared is nevertheless the *internal enemy*."[7]

The symbolic mortal here gets ahead of the physical mortal. Surviving so that one is not dead, although one could have or should have died (in the war), weighs as heavily, or even more heavily, than being dead and fading definitively into forgetfulness (in the depths of a cemetery). Even little Ernst, for whom it is discreetly mentioned in a note that his mother Sophie died as the manuscript was being written (1920), must "look death in the face," or bear an absence by recovering it in another presence. "Over there" (*Fort*) and "here" (*Da*). The reel in its back-and-forth surely figures the mother who is now distanced in her absence and invokes the desire for her return from work in the evening, but maybe also in what will later be a definitive disappearance. Consequently, the same "compulsion for repetition" is at play in the arising of traumatic memories of soldiers returning from the front as in the figured return of the lost-and-found by little Ernst.[8]

## The anorganic

But where does this game lead, and where does death go? This is the real question. For one can repeat endlessly the introduction of the death instinct on the side of or in combat with the "sexual drive" understood as a life instinct,[9] one understands its emergence only by relating it back to its originary state and final resting place—the "what" of the "It" that the "death drive" comes to designate—that is, the inorganic, or even better, the "anorganic" (*das Anorganische*) or the "lifeless" (*das Leblose*) for which we are fated:

> If we are to take it as a truth that knows no exception that everything living dies for internal reasons—*becomes anorganic once again* [*ins Anorganische zurückkehrt*]—then we shall be compelled to say that 'the aim of life is death' [*das Ziel alles Lebens ist der Tod*] and, looking backwards, that the *'lifeless'* [*das Leblose*] existed before the living.[10]

Thus, the "*anorganic*"—rather than the inorganic—as originary is the content of the Id that is woven into me from the start and awaits me at the end: the "lifeless" [*das Leblose*] that I was *before* and that I will be *again afterwards*. "What (then) is it?"—this absolute void, this hole, this hollow. It is *nothing*. Or at least *nothing* [*rien*] human, and yet *the nothing* [*le rien*] that constitutes us as such—not in a nothingness [*un néant*] that could still give meaning to my existence (Heidegger), but in an immemorial origin from whence we came and toward which we will return (Freud).

There is thus an underside of the "human," as I have said, and that is "animality." And there is an underside of "animality," as I have also stressed, and this is the "bestial." There is an underside of "bestiality," as I have just suggested, and it is the "brutal" or "becoming brutal" (de Lubac). Yet now there is also an underside of the "brutal," and that is the "lifeless," the "anorganic," or even the mineral as described here by Freud. Death is not only "dust" (Ecclesiastes) or the "disappearance of the self" (Heidegger) into a nothingness that gives meaning to life, but rather it is resistance to the Ego, a magma or Neuter beyond all meaningfulness, a descent to the lowest rung on the ladder of being—from the human to the animal, from the animal to the vegetable, from the vegetable to the mineral: "What I see is well *below the monkey*, on the *fringe of the vegetable world*, at the level of *jellyfish*."[11] Sartre's hero Antoine Roquentin as he looks into the mirror confesses in *Nausea* in a manner so astonishingly close to Freud's Id [*Ça*] that he even uses its name: "*It* [Ça] *is alive*, I can't say it isn't; but this was not the life that Anny contemplated...."[12]

The *lapidary*, in all senses of the term—the stone, surely, but also the cleaver—thus makes one *feel oneself living as dead*, even makes *one no longer feel at all*. Such is the odd experience that plagues every human. All attempts to elevate ourselves are only fictions or at least constructions, in respect to that to which we are tied to the self or by which we are afflicted within our very being. The church fathers of the desert (Evagrius of Pontus), of the Middle Ages (Thomas Aquinas) and the Renaissance (Charles de Bovelles), also knew this, and gave it a name: *acedia*, sometimes wrongly translated as sloth or melancholy. Etymologically, *acedia* is the absence of care (*akēdeo*), and it marks a state rather than a feeling. In the ladder of beings, it leads humans back or reduces them to the rank of the mineral, or in other words, to *stone* (*lapis*). A sort of forerunner to the death drive or to the reduction to the "anorganic" in Freud: the monk reaches *acedia*, and thus also a *draining*, as in the sense of the bay of Zuyderzee (we will come back to this), he no longer senses, no longer senses himself, nor senses that one senses him—be it man or God. As Charles de Bovelles, then canon of Noyons in the 15th century, notes:

Acedia [*acedia*] places man at the last rank and makes him similar to stones [*sicut mineralia*]. Just as these stones [*mineralia*], which remain fixed at the last order, possessing nothing other than their being such that to them there is neither given the exercise of the least natural function, nor any power to move in themselves, so also do those who possess this monstrous phenomenon of acedia sleep a dreamless sleep [*assiduo ferme somno consopescunt*], separated from all work [*ab actu omni et operatione remittuntur*], and made immobile like stones [*immoti ut lapides perstant*], as if mother nature had given them only being without any manifest force nor any power to act in a commendable manner.[13]

We can thus state it plainly: *spirituality and psychoanalysis* have something to exchange here, if only we do not confuse the aspirations of the first (the soul's straining toward God and its turning away into sin) with the specificity of the second (the quest solely for human depths). Like the death drive in Freud, the monk in the state of *acedia* is in some way held "outside of space" and "outside of time"—not at all in the sense of escaping from space and time, but rather in feeling oneself entirely "invaded" by space and time. It is not only this "void" or emptiness that causes suffering, because in the final analysis desire is always still present, or at least the possibility of filling it up. But it is rather and above all the "fullness," or even the "overfullness" (not of God but of self) that produces laziness, weariness, and exhaustion in the monk—to the point that nothing makes any sense, including the very idea of sense and non-sense. Presence is no longer a gift but rather a resistance.

In the "resistance of presence," the very idea of an absence as such becomes impossible, and so too does the impulse of desire. Acedia takes us "outside of time," or makes time endure in a duration that is not eternity, but is on the contrary, an infinite "persistence" that can never be suppressed or at least experienced as if it were written in temporality. Evagrius of Pontus, the initiator and founder of this sort of spirituality, says:

> The *demon* of *acedia*, also called the noonday demon, is the *most oppressive of all the demons*. He attacks the monk *about the fourth hour* and besieges his soul *until the eighth hour*. First of all, he makes *it appear that the sun moves slowly or not at all*, and that *the day seems to be fifty hours long*.[14]

In regard to both *acedia*, and the death drive in *Beyond the Pleasure Principle*, one would be wrong to interpret the Freudian "organic elasticity"[15]—which stretches the drive when it is directed toward life (life-drive) and relaxes it when it is directed toward death (death drive)—as a simple return to a stable state, a sort of absolute equilibrium, a state of repose or Nirvana—interpretations for which the father of psychoanalysis was wrongly reproached. This is the case because the question of the death drive does not refer to anxiety about tomorrow's death or yesterday's coming to life, and thus not about the worry engendered by the future or nostalgia for the past, but rather is about living in the present time that I traverse as a living or dying being, and thus as a being belonging or *already no longer* belonging to life: "We can live (in a melancholic manner) as if we were already dead... We just add now that even if the drive for repetition did not have as *its goal* this state of minimal tension that we have associated with death, it can very well have another sort of death as an effect, namely, that of the stifling of all creativity and thus of the meaning of life."[16]

In short, have we understood this much: "What is It?" in 1920, in *Beyond the Pleasure Principle*? It is certainly a force of life that is also opposed to a force of death or auto-destructivity. But only in this way does life "always tend toward death," and thus toward the Neutral, the mineral or the anorganic— naturally inscribed in the organic, and sometimes more accidentally arising in the psychic. The "Id" stands there before me, or better, below me, and supports the Ego. More radical than the "Khōra" as simple resistance (Derrida), more unformed than "raw nature" as element (Merleau-Ponty), the "Id" in some way is now turned toward the ego, toward me. It is *looking at me or concerns me*, it stares at me, it defies me, and it leads my Ego.

# Chapter Five

# It concerns me

There is "Nothing to It," certainly (the unformed underside of any aim or vision), but we must always "beware of It" (the brutality of the war, both internal and external), accept that "it's not nothing" (the drive on the border between the somatic and the psychic), and wonder "what is It?" (the anorganic, origin and fate of every living being). Yet none of this would matter were it not also my business. "It"—"*regards me*," that is to say, in the French sense, that "it knows me" or "it concerns me." This is the final stage by which the Id is given, to the extent that it can be given, or rather by which the "Id" resists and always remains beneath all givenness. In the second topography (Id, Ego, Superego), the borders are eliminated or at least relieved of the pretense of impermeability. The chaotic endlessly returns, emerges and sometimes submerges me, both before me and within me, by the greatest strangeness.

## Being lived

With *The Ego and the Id* in 1923—and although Freud finds himself suffering from cancer of the jaw—psychoanalysis has taken or at least embarks on a new turn. The anorganic character of the death drive in *Beyond the Pleasure Principle* (1920) had already reached the bottom of a chasm so that one might have believed to have touched its floor. But *The Ego and the Id* now requires us to go still deeper down, just as the thought and itinerary of the founder of psychoanalysis goes deeper still: "psychoanalysis has not hitherto shown its appreciation of certain things ... because it followed a particular path, *which had not yet led so far.*"[1] The earlier topography of the "Unconscious—Preconscious—Conscious" is no longer sufficient. It falls apart under the weight of the discovery of the death drive, seeks a new path, or better a radical recomposition: "In the further course of psycho-analytic work, however, even these distinctions have proved to be inadequate and, *for practical purposes*, insufficient."[2]

By deepening analytic practice, but also and especially under the shock of traumatic experiences (the Great War, the death of Sophie, jaw cancer), Freud gradually realizes that "what we call our ego behaves essentially passively in life" in the sense that "we *are lived* by unknown and uncontrollable forces."[3] This formulation, borrowed from Groddeck's *Book of the It*, demonstrates in some way that the "ego" no longer lives, or rather, that it *"is lived"*—hence the character of passivity and neutrality in its formulation (*das Es*). The anorganic character of the death drive (*Beyond the Pleasure Principle*) is here propelled into the quasi magma of the Id (*The Ego and the Id*). The odd schema of the "Id" depicted by Freud in *The Ego and the Id* makes this apparent. We know that the founder of psychoanalysis is a lover of "psychic geography." We thus see a kind of "Beyond the psyche" or an "Egg of the Id" to which the "ego" also belongs as its skin or surface, somewhat "like a germinal disk" decked out with a kind of "cap of hearing."[4] Such a drawing, at least by a child, surely makes one smile and shows at what point the Viennese thinker and doctor was marking out his path with the means available to him. Yet in the Id all is given or rather retained, and thus ready to erupt—or at least ready to let it be seen as being there, even if it is never truly seen or glimpsed: the unformed, the brutality of the war, the drive, the anorganic, and now the impersonal or the passivity of the Neuter.

We will therefore not, or no longer, say, as with the famous dictum from *Introductory Lectures on Psycho-Analysis* (1917), that the ego "is not even master in its own house,"[5] which still refers only to the first topography. With *The Ego and the Id* (1923), after the *Thoughts for the Present Times on War and Death* (1914), *The Drives and their Vicissitudes* (1916), *The Uncanny* (1920), and *Beyond the Pleasure Principle* (1920), we gradually and almost helplessly participate in a sort of "falling apart of the ego's house," or rather a spectacle of ruin that makes the house difficult to live in if not altogether uninhabitable. The ego is no longer "master of its own house," not because the house is totally destroyed or disorganized, or because certain corners of it remain hidden, but rather because I gradually come to feel uncanny, like "a stranger in my own home" (*das Unheimliche*).

## The knight of the Id

Yet as we must live, the ego will endeavor to mount its horse and stay in the saddle, according to the no less famous and remarkable, quasi equestrian, description of the joust of the Ego and the Id: "Thus in its relation to the id it is like *a man on horseback*, who has to hold in check the superior strength of the horse; with this difference, that the rider tries to do so with his own strength while the ego uses borrowed forces."[6]

Straddling the Id, the ego must therefore learn to leave it be, not in order to give up taming it or to abandon itself to it, but rather to wear out and deflect this force that outflanks it in order to advance itself and possibly to control it. There is a sort of "ruse of the Id" in Freud, like the good sailor who follows the wave in order to ride it, and even sometimes speeds into it rather than having it crash onto him. The knight himself will have a similar stratagem, playing the squire so as to not be thrown off his mount—like the psychoanalyst's stratagem to avoid losing himself or abandoning his patient on the couch: "Often a rider, if he is not to be parted from his horse, is obliged to guide it where it wants to go; so in the same way the ego is in the habit of *transforming* the id's will *into action as if* it were its own" says Freud in recognition less of its impotence than by the radicalization of its demand.[7]

## Being there for something

We would thus be wrong to believe that the ego is there for nothing, either as merely passive in a totally chaotic world, or as exclusively active in a total will to master everything. Neither psychoanalysis nor phenomenology is certainly and exclusively able to "dominate" everything (complete activity) or solely "let everything be" (pure passivity). "The other is the one who does not let me be," as Lévinas famously retorted against

Heideggerian *Gelassenheit*.[8] This is also true for the Id— both "a chaos of passions and drives" at the limit of the somatic and the psychic, and the indubitable horizon of death as a "formless" and lifeless world that nevertheless belongs to life. Getting out of and leaving behind the active-reactive opposition is probably truly what is at stake for *a phenomenology of force* inherited from Freud and Nietzsche. By itself, it will not be content merely to react or to increase, but it will finally agree that an energy could truly be released without always being recouped, even if for Freud it will be at least partially channeled: "Here we must note the immoderate taste of modern thought for this *reactive* aspect of forces." As Deleuze rightly notes in his still valid diagnostic reading of Nietzsche: "But it is also true that we can only grasp *reactive* forces for what they are, if we relate them *to what dominates them*, but is not itself *reactive*."[9]

# Chapter Six

# It touches me

*Where the Id was*

And so, this is how we hold onto the Id, or rather shows how we are held by and contained in it. Metaphor is surely the only way to get there, or let's say, to get close to it. The only way to the Id is exclusively by circumventing it rather than by a frontal attack. One says what it is by what it is not—but less this time in the beyond of an apophatic philosophy than via its resistance to discourse itself. Metaphor gestures not by explaining the Id but by featuring it. In a remarkable page from the *New Introductory Lectures on Psychoanalysis* (1932), Freud suggests:

> We approach the id with analogies: we call it *chaos, a cauldron full of seething excitations*. We picture it as being *open at its end to somatic influences*, and as

there taking up into itself instinctual needs which find their psychical expression in it, but *we cannot say in what substratum….* *The logical laws of thought* do not apply to the id, and this is true above all of the law of contradiction…. There is nothing in the id that could be compared with *negation* [….] There is nothing in the id that corresponds to the *idea of time* [….] The id of course knows *no judgement of value*: no good and evil, no morality…. *Where id was, there ego shall be.* It is a work of culture—not unlike the draining of the Zuyderzee.[1]

Nearly everything is said about the Id here, as a "cauldron full of seething excitement" (Freud) and a "Chaos of our passions and drives" (*Wedding Feast of the Lamb*); or of the non-linguistic or even infra-linguistic Id (Freud) to the "realm of what we can no longer say," to the *Khōra* or to the "battle of sensations" (*The Loving Struggle*). In the framework of psychoanalysis, the Id reaches what we were already looking for in philosophical terms, even if awkwardly.[2] There is in us this "dark, inaccessible part of our personality,"[3] to borrow Freud's other determination of the Id, which results not only in us not seeing it, but also in us not looking for it.[4] *There is nothing to see*, certainly, insofar as the Id is not seen and is of a wholly different order, but this does not prohibit us from looking for it, quite to the contrary. The obscurity here is not such that it exceeds or overwhelms us, like the "more than luminous shadow of silence" (Dionysius) about which we could say nothing except that we cannot say anything about it. Far from any negative theology or philosophy, as I have said, the Id is "resistance" to a power (the ego and its will to direct) rather than a "remainder" of a dependency (God or the beyond of discourse). Not merely unassimilated, it is also unassimilable, and thus impregnable. *Neither* logic *nor* negation, *neither* judgment of value *nor* representation of time, the Id does not belong to privation or to the beyond of discourse—which would still attribute too much to it in the form of a relic of givenness—but it is properly speaking "Extra-phenomenal" or "expropriation": not unrepresentable but escaping from and even destroying the very idea of representation.[5]

## *The draining of the Zuyderzee*

This "cultural work"—in the form of the "draining of the Zuyderzee," i.e., as the *sea that lets the earth appear*—will surely make the ground visible by trying to make the tumult recede. "Where id was, there ego shall be"—*Wo es war, soll ich werden*— according to Freud's famous formulation.[6] We will always take a "wager on meaning," and this is probably the incessant avowal of the ego on the surface of the id. It seems as if one had sunk or must founder, but in most cases the Ego submerged in the Id manages to float, and sometimes even to breathe and swim:

> The ego is after all only *a portion of the id*, a portion that has been expediently modified by the proximity of the external world with its threat of danger. ... it has borrowed its energies from the id, and we are not entirely without insight into the *methods*—we might call them *dodges*—by which it *extracts* further amounts of energy *from the id*.[7]

It is thus useless to wallow in a Magma whose decompression or even suffocation led to the speechlessness or pure presence of trauma. The ego (or the superego) does not negate the Id, "the super-ego *merges* into the id," to borrow Freud's very words.[8] Definitively warned against all false bids or temptations of the impermeability of the psychic spheres, the psychoanalyst gradually recognizes their instability and sees how we are "engraved by the Id" in the whole of our being. The world is made of "chiasm," "transition," "interlacing" and "entanglement" according to a lesson that Merleau-Ponty himself probably received from Freud. Far from any declarations in the form of ruptures, from the overcoming of metaphysics or the opening to another discourse, Freud already knew or progressively learned through a sort of pilgrimage in psychoanalysis that the "pure" or the "without mixture" belongs neither to reality nor to proposals one could make about it. This is also true for the psychic spheres, and for existence as such, wherein any compartmentalization ignores the "seams" or the "play" that allow fields to communicate, to glide along the terrain and sometimes to cross over into each other, to the point of no longer knowing which possesses what property or claim to exclusivity. As Freud explains in no less magisterial fashion in the 1932 lecture:

> In thinking of this division of the personality into an ego, a super-ego and an id, you will not, of course, have pictured sharp frontiers like the artificial ones drawn in political geography. We cannot do justice to the characteristics of the mind by linear outlines like those in a drawing or in primitive painting, but rather by areas of colour melting into one another as

they are presented by modern artists. After making the separation we must allow what we have separated to merge together once more.[9]

## The great cavalcade

Because nothing is fixed and borders never stop moving, because political geography has nothing in common with psychic geography—I will say that "*it touches me*"—at least in the sense that "it affects me." The Id touches me—in the psychic sense but perhaps also in the "sensual" or "sensational" meaning of the term—certainly and first of all because the Id disturbs me, does not leave me alone in my ego, and plays with my *pathos*, whether in joy or suffering. The knight should "lead the horse," to return to the metaphor borrowed from Freud, "determine the goal to be reached" and "guide the movement of the powerful animal." Yet as the father of psychoanalysis is now obliged to recognize, "only too often there arises between the ego and the id the *not precisely ideal situation* of the rider being obliged to guide the horse along the path by which *it itself wants to go.*"[10] In one great ride, the knight sometimes embarks where he doesn't want or didn't plan to go. The Knight of the Id, in *The Ego and the Id* (1923), is as if unhorsed nearly ten years later, in *New Introductory Lectures on Psychoanalysis* (1932). Freud's effort and attempt to radicalize never stops getting deeper, such that "affect"—and it alone—gradually becomes that which guides me.[11]

But the Id also touches or affects me, and perhaps even more so because the Id has moved the lines, broken the dams, and destroyed or eliminated the barriers, much like *modern* fauvist or impressionist *painting* of that period, in which there are no more "straight lines" but encounters are created with "areas of color."[12] In short, one had duly "separated" and methodologically "dissected" in psychoanalytic theory (the first topography) and also in philosophy—and maybe more in phenomenology than elsewhere (reduction, variation, description). Maybe it is now time to bring them back together thanks to the "attack" or "backlash" of psychoanalysis on phenomenology. The instability of the Id requires not to remain "there," or at the "there" of the separation of borders and strict delimitation of fields. One "crosses the Rubicon" from phenomenology into theology, and vice versa, but also from phenomenology into psychoanalysis, and vice versa. It is by learning and by being modified by its "other" that phenomenology will advance and will stop condemning every other science as "ontic." And it is by descending ever further into the depths of the self—of the human surely but also of the world and even of God—that it will attain the depths where perhaps it has not yet arrived.

"We would give much to understand more about these things!"[13] Freud exclaims while following the meandering descriptions of the Id and recognizing in conclusion that such developments are "exacting and not, perhaps, very illuminating."[14] In sum, it matters little that we do not know "everything," and sometimes it is probably better to know "nothing." Yet, if one does not say everything of the "nothing," one also does not say "nothing." For the Id does not see anything [*"Ça" ne voit rien*]—*there is nothing to it* [Ça n'a rien à voir]—not because it exceeds us but because it resists us. Thus we must turn *around* the Id, draw its contours in order to get closer to it, but without letting ourselves be consumed by it. It is only at this price that one can let the Id emerge, paid for by the "ego" or a "divine form" to effect its "salvation" and blessing—provided this were necessary, and by being careful not to face it alone, or at least not to avoid it.

# What's God have to do with it?

*For the salvation of the Id*

> The relation to the external world has become the decisive factor for the ego; it has taken on the task of representing the external world to the id—*for the salvation of the Id.*[1]

Freud's formulation, once again excerpted from the *New Introductory Lectures on Psychanalysis* in 1932, is certainly astonishing. Would the Id need *salvation* or need to be *saved?* This Id—which is in each of us and within which we are held—would it not be interested in *getting along with another,* if not to express itself, then at least so as not to be "alone" in the "formlessness of the lifeless" or in the "bubbling cauldron of excitations" that each of us is? Paradoxically, one needs an Ego for the Id not to be left to itself—with the inverse risk of the ego getting lost in excessive solitude. Being too separated creates the hegemony of a world that believes in total domination, yet its desert only reinforces the inability of something all-powerful to exert itself: "the id ... could not escape *destruction if*, in its blind efforts for the satisfaction of its instincts, it disregarded that *supreme external power*."[2]

That the Id has "to be saved" obviously does not mean that one would find in it some trace of fault or sin, which has no place in psychoanalysis. But one would demand—just once won't hurt—that it cooperate or find another, including in its claim to govern everything. The Id needs the Ego not to exist but better to manifest itself, including in exteriority. It seeks "representatives" and "proxies" or "emissaries" so that the "distance of thought" is established less in order to tame it than to exhibit it *differently*: "*The ego controls* the approaches to motility *under the id's orders*; but between a need and an action it has interposed a postponement in the form of *the activity of thought*...."[3] In brief, the Id is *no longer alone* or does not stand *alone*, and this is perhaps also the "salvation of the Id."[4]

## Apart from it

"Life is not easy!" Freud exclaims[5]—and we have seen how this applies to the probable link between *his* life and the deepening and radicalization of psychoanalysis. One should thus not rush to saying that "things will work out [*ça ira, ça ira*]" just to save the Id. For if the ego really goes together with the id, it will no longer be thought *on its own* [à part *soi*] or even otherwise [*à part ça*]. This is Freud's great originality. The ego is never nourished by a too easily conquered or falsely pacified unity. The ego always remains "in struggle," insofar as not all "combat" (*agon*) is necessarily a "war" (*polemos*). One can "be" and even "become" oneself in undertaking positive struggle—whether the ego and the id are at stake or me and the other: "I will not let you go lest you bless me," says Jacob in his struggle with the angel (Genesis 32:26). Nevertheless, sometimes the dam breaks and borders disappear—or "areas of color" merge so much that only a "shared ground" remains—or sometimes an "odious mixture" in which nothing can be distinguished anymore, not even the possibility of formulating anything. The admission of *the ego's weakness*, or the *onset of anxiety*, has nothing to do with any psychologism here, but instead testifies to the ontological and existential ground of the human as such. The Id will be less denied or obliterated like the "nothing" in Heideggerian angst than it will be manifested, even exacerbated, in its pure presence:

> Thus the ego, *driven* by the id, *confined* by the super-ego, repulsed by reality, *struggles* to master its economic task... If the ego is *obliged to admit its weakness, it breaks out in anxiety*—realistic anxiety regarding the external world, moral anxiety regarding the super-ego and neurotic anxiety regarding the strength of the passions in the id.[6]

### The realm of the Id

And so, "what's God have to do with it?" This is a surprising question, especially as nothing induces it—especially not the

Id. Nothing demands a god, or even the name of God. One could remain "human *without* God," as I have sufficiently shown elsewhere, without being *against* God, just by simply living *our incarnated self,* provided that it is God's very goal not only to raise us up, but also to call us to "be with him" in our shared humanity.[7] What's true for the "spiritual" is also true for the "carnal," even for the "physical" as such: one is *raised up* only in *being abased*—or rather, the more one climbs and the more one weighs, the more one is drawn down, according to the most basic law of gravity. In short, and this will be the final lesson of psychoanalysis for phenomenology: there is no "*beyond*" without a descent into the "*below*," nor is there any *transcendence* without first anchoring or rooting it in *immanence*.

So if there is a God, or if we can have an experience "of God," he would not only (and not solely) hover in the cloud of a sovereign distanced Good (Dionysius), but also in the lowliness and humility of the incarnated Word (Bonaventure). After the God of the "descent into Khōra" (Derrida) and then the "savage God" (Merleau-Ponty),[8] next and curiously there is the *"God of the Id"* or the *"Id of God"* (Freud), in so far as nothing—including our "bubbling cauldron" or the "anorganic" of death—can escape from a conception of the divine whose first ambition is to take on or shoulder everything or even to transform everything.

*(Die) dunkle Wahrnehmung jenseits des Ich(s), des Reichs des Es*—"Mysticism is the obscure *self-perception* of the *realm* outside of the *ego*, of the *id*."[9] And so with this enigmatic note from August 22, 1938, nearly on the eve of his death (on September 23, 1939 in London), the whole of Freud's work is achieved. A "*mystical* realm of the Id," or a "*realm of the Id* on the order of the mystical"—it doesn't matter. No one will know what this is

really all about, perhaps not even the author of the formulation himself. All the same, the thing is there, if not said then at least written. *"God in It/Id all"* is certainly not everything, yet it is probably also not nothing. Perhaps it can be properly defined, according to an aim that will reunite the attempts I have here secretly interwoven by this unique but exemplary capacity to join us back together again, or to *"be with us"* in the "Id."[10]

# Regarding all of it

Regarding "all of it,"—was *psychoanalysis* worth it or was it ever worth "an hour of trouble"—to borrow Pascal's famous confrontation with philosophy in the encounter with Descartes?[1] Most certainly, at least in my view, and there was no little trouble involved, as for any neophyte who, to become acquainted with a subject matter, knows that in order to advance, or better, to descend, some day or other he or she must come back up. The essential is not only to come back to the surface, but not to venture alone into one's own underground, as is true both for the "trial of the body" and the "ethics of the spread body."[2] This, probably, is *salvation*—of the Id, surely, but also of the human as such. Not to flee our humanity or even our animality, our bestiality or our "becoming brute," our "mineralization" or our "anorganic"—but also not "to stand alone" in it, because in "being at least two in oneself," one can already be considered saved.

To bring the Enlightenment to an end, to conceive the inconceivable, to be rooted in the organic, not to fear the uncanny, to go all the way to the anorganic, to be lived by the Id, to want to be its knight and recognize in the end that one risks embarking on a great ride—such is the path lived simultaneously by Freud himself, and through him, the history of the development of psychoanalysis. No thought is ever separated or abstracted from the mode of life from which it emerged. This is where this *philosophical reading of Freud* will have led us, for the good of psychoanalysis perhaps (that's not for me to judge), but certainly for the good of philosophy. It was necessary to renew the long-abandoned dialogue starting from where Ricœur, Derrida, Foucault, or Henry had long practiced it. This modest essay will at least be an attempt to do so, if only in order to trace out a path that is still to be cleared.

The program of the "backlash of psychoanalysis onto phenomenology" remains far from being complete and other works (or the works of others) could potentially complement it. The essential work has nevertheless been done, or rather said, by which phenomenology will inherit from psychoanalysis—not falsely to baptize the psychic but to *orient differently* its own "descent into the abyss," or what one might call its "kenotic ambition." We will have at least discovered by this foray the nugget or precious stone that we know we had to seek, at the risk of never finding or even suspecting it. Such are the stakes of every quest and of every "entry into abysses" that phenomenology must now try to bring about. As Merleau-Ponty tells us in a final effort to give phenomenology a new program:

Since our philosophy has given us no better way to express that *intemporal,* that *indestructible* element in us which, says Freud, is the unconscious itself, perhaps we should continue calling it the unconscious—so long as we do not forget that the word is the index of an enigma—because the term retains, like the algae or the stone that one drags up, something of the sea from which it was taken.[3]

# Notes

## Foreword

1   Merleau-Ponty, "The Primacy of Perception and its Philosophical Consequences," in *The Merleau-Ponty Reader*, Northwestern University Studies in Phenomenology & Existential Philosophy (Evanston, Ill.: Northwestern University Press, 2007), 100-01.

2   Maurice Merleau-Ponty, "Phenomenology and Psychoanalysis: Preface to Hesnard's *L'Œuvre de Freud*," in *The Essential Writings of Merleau-Ponty*, trans. Alden L. Fisher (New York: Harcourt, Brace & World, 1969), 85, translation modified.

## Opening Act: Philosophizing in psychoanalysis

1   Paul Ricœur, "A Philosophical Interpretation of Freud," trans. Willis Domingo, in *The Conflict of Interpretations: Essays in Hermeneutics*, ed. Don Ihde (Evanston, Ill.: Northwestern University Press, 1974 and 2007), 160; emphasis added.

2   Ibid., 159-60; emphasis added.

3   I am here referring to my work and hypothesis in *Crossing the Rubicon: The Borderlands of Philosophy and Theology*, trans. Reuben Shank (New York: Fordham University Press, 2016). The present work applies the term in regard to the relation of

philosophy to psychoanalysis. As for the "turn," at least as concerns the relation of phenomenology to theology, see Dominique Janicaud, *Phenomenology and the "Theological Turn": The French Debate*, trans. Bernard G. Prusak (New York: Fordham University Press, 2000).

4   The present essay—*Nothing to It*—is situated in a position of both proximity and distance relative to the work of Michel Henry. Its proximity is found in my agreement with *The Essence of Manifestation* in affirming with Novalis' "Hymn to the Night" that: "the Night is not merely opposed to the light of day; it is not merely its privation." Michel Henry, *The Essence of Manifestation*, trans. Gerard Etzkorn (The Hague: Nijhoff, 1973), §50, 442. The distance is found in ceasing to think that "the night accomplishes the work of revelation" (ibid., 441) or, further, that "this absence of the world and of its light… is *not the absence of phenomenality*" (ibid., 442; emphasis in the original). This is because the "Id" as we will show, "does not give something to be seen," and therefore it does not phenomenalize itself. The *a priori of phenomenalization*, not only in its actuality but also in its possibility, is what "my philosophical reading of Freud" will come to challenge for phenomenology itself. I will therefore no longer follow Michel Henry in his *The Genealogy of Psychoanalysis*, trans. Douglas Brick (Stanford, Calif.: Stanford University Press, 1993), in the condemnation of the unconscious, and probably the entirety of psychoanalysis "as the ultimate illusion of representational metaphysics" (ibid., 318). Because saying that "*the unconscious does not escape from every form of phenomenality* but within *ek-stasis is the site of the first appearance*, of its self-appearing as life and affectivity," (ibid., 316.), and adding that "Freud unintentionally recognizes the fact" (ibid.), possibly depends on the "first topography," (as Metapsychology is here invoked by Henry), but not on "the second" (which precisely, and by the "Id," relieves the unconscious of any "possibility of appearing"). For what counts is not the "aim" of the phenom-

enologist upon the unconscious from the presupposition of intentionality—even if it is reduced to a "radical (i.e., material) phenomenology" (ibid., 321.)—but rather it is the "backlash" of psychoanalysis on phenomenology itself, regarding this never interrogated a priori of manifestation and its possible signification. Michel Henry's preemptory judgment against psychoanalysis is understandable, according to which "that 'obscure recognition… of the unconscious,' its affectivity, *overturns the entire dogmatic apparatus of Freudianism*. They designate it as *a thought of life that was incapable of equaling its project*" (ibid., 316), but *even as phenomenologist* I do not share it. One should not be satisfied with accusing Freud for not having gone where he should have, starting with the already traced out intention of an experience of the self with no other objective than for it to manifest itself. Trauma breaks the very possibility of visibility, and even of grasping the invisible. For the true night, the "other night," to say it with Maurice Blanchot, is not the "phenomenology of night" (a perspective shared with Novalis' "Hymn to the Night" and Michel Henry after him), but the "night of phenomenology" (which is shown, for example, by Maurice Blanchot's *Thomas the Obscure* or by Emmanuel Lévinas' commentary on it in his *Existence and Existents*, trans. Alphonso Lingis [Dordrecht/London: Kluwer, 1988], 62-63). For more on this distinction see my own contribution entitled "The Extra-Phenomenal," *Diakrisis. Yearbook of Theology and Philosophy* I (2018).

5    Maurice Merleau-Ponty, *Phenomenology of Perception*, trans. Donald A. Landes (New York: Routledge, 2012), 160.

6    Merleau-Ponty, "The Primacy of Perception and its Philosophical Consequences," in *The Merleau-Ponty Reader*, Northwestern University Studies in Phenomenology & Existential Philosophy (Evanston, Ill.: Northwestern University Press, 2007), 100-01.

7    Merleau-Ponty, "The Philosopher and Sociology," in *Signs*, trans. Richard C. McCleary (Evanston, Ill.: Northwestern Uni-

versity Press, 1964), 98.

[8]    Merleau-Ponty *"Les sciences de l'homme et la phénoménologie,"* in *Merleau-Ponty à la Sorbonne. Résumé de cours 1949-1952* (Grenoble: Cynara, 1988), 422.

[9]    Ibid. See also Merleau-Ponty, "The Philosopher and Sociology," in *Signs*, 128f. For "The Interlacing—Chiasm" being transposed to the relation of phenomenology and psychoanalysis, see Merleau-Ponty, *The Visible and the Invisible; Followed by Working Notes*, trans. Alphonso Lingis (Evanston Ill.: Northwestern University Press, 1968), 130-162. This praise would not have been possible without the careful introduction by Emmanuel de Saint-Aubert, "La psychologie entrelacée à la philosophie," in *Vers une ontologie fondamentale. Sources et enjeux critiques de l'appel à l'ontologie chez Merleau-Ponty* (Paris: J. Vrin, 2006), 81-89.

[10]   See Paul Ricœur, *Freud and Philosophy: An Essay on Interpretation*, trans. Denis Savage (New Haven: Yale University Press, 1970), 378. He continues: "A second step toward the Freudian unconscious is represented by the notion of intentionality, a notion both commonplace and unfathomable." Although Ricœur does not reduce psychoanalysis to phenomenology ("Phenomenology is a reflexive discipline…. Psychoanalysis is not a reflexive discipline…." ibid., 390.), the *signifying* aim remains from start to finish what guides the whole work in the quest for "interpretation"—thereby diverging largely from the perspective envisaged here. Less than an opposition, I see here instead two different perspectives: on the one hand in the "clarification" of phenomenology starting from psychoanalysis (Ricœur), and on the other in the "backlash" of psychoanalysis on phenomenology (the present work).

[11]   Edmund Husserl, *Cartesian Meditations: An Introduction to Phenomenology*, trans. Dorion Cairns (The Hague: M. Nijhoff, 1960), § 16, 38-39; translation modified.

12    Merleau-Ponty, *Phenomenology of Perception*, 160-61. This is a reference to Sigmund Freud's, "Introductory Lectures on Psycho-Analysis (1916-1917[1915-1917]), in *The Standard Edition of the Complete Psychological Works of Sigmund Freud* trans. James Strachey, vol. XV (London: The Hogarth Press and the Institute of Psycho-analysis, 1991), 60-61.

13    Merleau-Ponty, "The Primacy of Perception," in *The Merleau-Ponty Reader* (Evanston, Ill.: Northwestern University Press, 2007), 105f.; emphasis added.

14    See my chapter, "A Phenomenology of the Underground: Maurice Merleau-Ponty," in *The Loving Struggle: Phenomenological and Theological Debates*, trans. Bradley B. Onishi and Lucas McCracken (Lanham: Rowman & Littlefield International, 2018), 67-110.

15    Maurice Merleau-Ponty, "Phenomenology and Psychoanalysis: Preface to Hesnard's *L'Œuvre de Freud*," in *The Essential Writings of Merleau-Ponty*, trans. Alden L. Fisher (New York: Harcourt, Brace & World, 1969), 85; translation modified. Paul Ricœur, for his part, already seems to have seen this, citing precisely this preface by Merleau-Ponty as the source for a return to the chaotic, or even to the primitive, within psychoanalysis via the detour through phenomenology: "The theme of *anteriority* pervades Freudianism. I would defend it against all the culturalisms which have tried to extract its fangs and pull its claws by reducing to defects of our current relationship to the environment the savage side of our instinctual existence...." (*The Conflict of Interpretations*, 169-70). But immediately this reduces the return to chaos to the concept of *archeology*, defined here as "reflexive"—which is not, strictly speaking, Maurice Merleau-Ponty's aim, whatever Paul Ricœur may say: "But we must see the concept of *archaeology* as itself a *reflexive* concept. Archaeology is the archaeology of the subject." This is what Merleau-Ponty saw and said clearly in his Preface to the work of Dr. Hesnard,

*L'Œuvre de Freud*" (*Essential Writings*, 170). On the whole, Freud's "reflexive" aim, as I have emphasized in this text (note 10, pg. 106), is founded exclusively upon "interpretation" and the investigation of "meaning" as is confirmed in Ricœur's chapter, "Reflection: An Archeology of the Subject," in *Freud and Philosophy*, 419-57.

16  See the working notes (February 1959), in *The Visible and the Invisible*, 180: "This unconscious is to be sought not at the bottom of ourselves, behind the back of our 'consciousness,' but in front of us, as articulations of our field. It is 'unconscious' by the fact that it is not an *object*, but it is that through which objects are possible, it is the constellation wherein our future is read...."

17  See the section "From the Threshold to the Leap," in the chapter "The Limited Phenomenon," in my *Crossing the Rubicon*, 145-47.

18  Georg Groddeck, *The Book of the It: Psychoanalytic Letters to a Friend* (London: Daniel, 1935). This work is at the origin of Freud's second topography (Id-Ego-Superego).

19  *The Essential Writings of Merleau-Ponty*, 87.

## Introduction: Go take a look

1  It can therefore be said that this text is founded upon two of my earlier works, and if not a sequel, it is at least a deepening of the same aim: see especially the first chapter, "Khōra or the Great Bifurcation: Jacques Derrida," and also chapter two, "A Phenomenology of the Underground: Maurice Merleau-Ponty," in *The Loving Struggle*, 19-44 and 45-75. This is in addition to the first part "Descent into the Abyss," from *The Wedding Feast of the Lamb: Eros, the Body, and the Eucharist*, trans. George Hughes (New York, NY: Fordham University Press, 2016), 5-58.

2  Henri Maldiney, "Existence; crise et création," in *Maldiney. Une singulière présence* (France: Éditions les belles lettres, 2014), 219-

57. See the distinction between the "pathic" and the "patho-logical": "To the reifying opposition of the normal and the pathological, there must succeed the existential articulation of the pathic and pathological," the recognition of the "crisis" or the "pathic" as the mark of life itself, and its absence as the place of the "pathological," and also that "the mark of the pathologic-al, it is not the crisis but on the contrary its impossibility" (ibid., 221).

3   Sabine Fos-Falque, *Comme en miroir. Les bruits de l'inconscient* (Paris: Cerf, 2018), 18: "The consciousness of being there with oneself without any possibility of being elsewhere besides one-self contains thought as much as it constrains it. It is thus with-out recourse to another horizon. To be one's self is as much a base as a limitation."

## Chapter One: Keep moving, nothing to see

1   Maurice Merleau-Ponty, "Phenomenology and Psychoanalysis: Preface to Hesnard's *L'Œuvre de Freud*," in *The Essential Writings of Merleau-Ponty*, 85-86; emphasis added.

2   Sigmund Freud, "The Future Prospects of Psycho-Analytic Therapy (1910)," in *The Standard Edition of the Complete Psych-ological Works of Sigmund Freud*, trans. James Strachey, vol. XI (London: The Hogarth Press and the Institute of Psycho-analy-sis, 1986), 151; translation modified (with the term *Aufklärung* rather than illumination). This is cited and analyzed by Lau-rence Kahn, *Faire parler le destin* (Paris: Klincksieck, 2005), 8.

3   Sigmund Freud, "Moses and Monotheism: Three Essays (1939 [1934-38]) in *The Standard Edition of the Complete Psychological Works of Sigmund Freud* trans. James Strachey, vol. XXIII (Lon-don: The Hogarth Press and the Institute of Psycho-analysis, 1991), 54; emphasis added.

4    Emmanuel Levinas, *Totality and Infinity: An Essay on Exteriority*, trans. Alphonso Lingis (The Hague: M. Nijhoff Publishers 1979), 124, 294, 34, and 56. "Clarity is the disappearance of what could shock" and "the Heideggerian thesis that every human attitude consists in 'bringing to light'… rests on this primacy of the panoramic" and also that "by the caress," "the essentially hidden throws itself toward the light, *without becoming signification*." On Emmanuel Lévinas' major calling into question of the phenomenological pattern of focusing on "light," see the very suggestive book by Marc-Alain Ouaknin, *Méditations érotiques. Essai sur Emmanuel Levinas* (Paris: Balland, 1992), 42. In particular his remark that "the phenomenology of eros in Lévinas—the only chapter in Lévinas' entire work that contains the word phenomenology ["Beyond the Face," in *Totality and Infinity*]—is a radical critique of the phenomenological project, both Husserlian as much as Heideggerian."

5    See Merleau-Ponty, *The Visible and the Invisible*, 147. He states: "My left hand is always on the verge of touching my right hand touching the things, but I never reach coincidence…" He inherits this from Edmund Husserl's *Ideas II*: "The indicational sensations of movement and the representational sensations of touch, which are objectified as features of the thing, 'left hand,' belong in fact to my right hand." Edmund Husserl, *Ideas Pertaining to a Pure Phenomenology and to a Phenomenological Philosophy: Second Book. Studies in the Phenomenology of Constitution*, trans. Richard Rojcewicz and André Schuwer (Dordrecht/ Boston: Kluwer Academic, 1989), §36, 152.

6    See my work, "The Gaps of the Flesh," in *The Wedding Feast of the Lamb*, §24, 166-72.

7    See Maurice Merleau-Ponty, "Dialogue and the Perception of the Other," in *The Prose of the World*, trans. John O'Neill (Evanston: Northwestern University Press, 1973), 135: "It is no longer enough for me to feel: I feel that someone feels me, that he

feels both my feeling and my feeling the very fact that he feels me…. The mystery of the other is nothing but the mystery of myself."

8    Sigmund Freud, "Papers on Metapsychology [1915]," in *The Standard Edition of the Complete Psychological Works of Sigmund Freud*, vol. XIV (London: The Hogarth Press and the Institute of Psycho-analysis, 1991), 173.

9    Ibid., 177; emphasis added.

10    Ibid., 193.

11    Sigmund Freud, "Thoughts for the Times on War and Death (1915)," 275.

12    Ibid., 278; translation modified.

13    He says: "The evil of loneliness is *not the fact of it being found in the world*, but *evil by the very fact of it being in itself*." Emmanuel Lévinas, *Carnets de captivité et autres inédits, Œuvres I* (Paris: B. Grasset, 2009), 52; emphasis added. This subject is covered in my essay "Evil and Finitude," in Bruce Ellis Benson and B. Keith Putt, eds, *Evil, Fallenness, and Finitude* (Cham, Switzerland: Palgrave Macmillan, 2017), 77-96.

## Chapter Two: Beware of it

1    On this point see Roger Bruyeron's very instructive work: *1914. L'entrée en guerre de quelques philosophes. Edmund Husserl, Henri Bergson, Bertrand Russell, Sigmund Freud* (Paris: Hermann, 2014), 17. He says: "There was no shortage of enthusiasts in Europe during the summer of 1914 and especially with the announcement of the declarations of war. It seems to me that *Husserl* yielded to this 'mystique': of all the philosophers, he is probably the one who was *closest* to this common sentiment." This is evidenced by the correspondence between Edmund Husserl and Heinrich Husserl (letter from August 8th, 1914): "And then

this seriousness, this resolute resolve, this joy and this calm! These are intense moments. Everything is filled with the spirit of patriotism and tears" (ibid., 91); From the letter of September 19th, 1914: "The parade in rank of battalions was a great event for the city, as most of the volunteers came from here: these 500 admirable young people were covered with flowers" (ibid., 95). An enthusiasm that will be undermined, of course, by the death of Edmund Husserl's son, Wolfgang, who fell on the front at Verdun, on March 8th, 1916 (ibid., 84).

2    Sigmund Freud, Ernst Pfeiffer, and Lou Andreas-Salomé, *Sigmund Freud and Lou Andreas-Salomé: Letters*, trans. William and Elaine Robson Scott (London: Hogarth Press: Institute of Psycho-analysis, 1972), 20; translation lightly modified; emphasis added.

3    Sigmund Freud, "Thoughts for the Times on War and Death (1915)," in *The Standard Edition of the Complete Psychological Works of Sigmund Freud*, XIV, 278-79; emphasis added.

4    Sigmund Freud, "Letter from November 25th, 1914," in *Sigmund Freud and Lou Andreas-Salomé: Letters*, 21; emphasis added.

5    Sigmund Freud, "Thoughts for the Times on War and Death (1915)," in *The Standard Edition of the Complete Psychological Works of Sigmund Freud*, XIV, 291-92.

6    Ibid., 287, 296; emphasis added.

7    Ibid., 285.

8    Ibid., 297; emphasis added.

9    Franz Rosenzweig, *The Star of Redemption*, trans. Barbara E. Galli (Madison, Wis.: University of Wisconsin Press, 2005), 9; translation modified; emphasis added.

10    Ibid. The perspective of "absolute evil" here, as destroying the very possibility of suffering it or of permitting it to emerge in an horizon, is taken up by Emmanuel Lévinas, although for him in regard to the Second World War (39-45)—and again, here is where the "neutral" or the "anonymous" is found, no longer the "It" (psychoanalysis), but the "there is" (phenomenology). See Levinas, *Existence and Existents*, 58: "In the night, where we are riven to it, we are not dealing with anything. But this nothing is not that of pure nothingness. There is no longer *this* or *that*; there is not 'something.' But this universal absence is in its turn a presence, an absolutely unavoidable presence.... *There is,* in general without it mattering what there is, without our being able to fix a substantive to this term. *There is* is an impersonal form, like in it rains, or it is warm. Its anonymity is essential." See my own contribution on this point in the essay, "Evil and Finitude," in Benson, *Evil, Fallenness, and Finitude*, 77-96.

11    Rosenzweig, *The Star of Redemption*, 103-21.

12    Ibid., 9.

13    Henri de Lubac, *Pic de la Mirandole. Études et discussions* (Paris: Aubier Montaigne, 1974), 202. The succession of humanity to animality, and then from animality to bestiality is studied in the chapter, "The Other Side of the Angel," in my text *The Wedding Feast of the Lamb*, §13, 70-8. In order to radicalize the passage from bestiality to brutality, or even brutality to the inorganic (infra), descending ever further into the Id, there is maybe a need to not lock oneself within it.

14    That the "self" for Nietzsche (*das Selbst*) is not exactly the "Id" for Freud or for Groddeck, see Rosenzweig (*das Es*). This is a distinction that I cannot elaborate here in the context of this simple analysis of the "Id" in Freud. However, the same neutrality, even resistance to meaning, is discovered in the same way for both. See Friedrich Nietzsche, *Thus Spoke Zarathustra*, trans. Adrian

Del Caro (Cambridge: Cambridge University Press, 2006), 23: "The self says to the ego: *Feel pain here!* And then it suffers and reflects on how it might suffer no more—and just for that purpose *it is supposed* to think. The self says to the ego: *'Feel pleasure here!'* Then it is pleased and reflects on how it might feel pleased more often—and for that purpose *it is supposed* to think!"

## Chapter Three: It's not nothing

1  This is an expression that refers to the French soldiers going to the war with "flowers on their rifles" and in "red pants," a uniform not adapted to the violence of combat "in the lowlands" (Verdun).

2  Sigmund Freud, "Papers on Metapsychology [1915]," in *The Standard Edition of the Complete Psychological Works of Sigmund Freud*, XIV, 121-22; translation modified.

3  "Dasein is an entity which, in its very Being, comports itself understandingly towards that Being.... Dasein [alone] *exists*." Martin Heidegger, *Being and Time*, trans. Joan Stambaugh (Albany, NY: State University of New York Press, 1996), §12, 78 [S.53]; emphasis added.

4  Karl Jaspers, *Autobiographie philosophique*, trans. Pierre Boudot (Paris: Aubier, 1963), 193. He says: "It is first of all in the limit situations that man becomes aware of his being .... This was one of the reasons why I chose medicine and psychiatry; I wanted to know *the limit where human possibilities fail*, to understand the meaning of what the public does not admit and of which it does not see the importance."

5  Sigmund Freud, "Papers on Metapsychology [1915]," in *The Standard Edition of the Complete Psychological Works of Sigmund Freud*, XIV, 123; translation lightly modified; emphasis added.

6  Jacques Lacan, *The Ego in Freud's Theory and in the Technique of Psychoanalysis, 1954-1955*, trans. Sylvana Tomaselli, vol. II,

*The Seminar of Jacques Lacan* (New York, N.Y.: W.W. Norton, 1988), 97.

7    Rudolf Bernet, *Force-pulsion-désir. Une autre philosophie de la psychanalyse*, Problèmes et controverses (Paris: J. Vrin, 2013), 240.

8    Falque, "The Limit of the Phenomenon," *The Wedding Feast of the Lamb*, §3, 18-24.

9    See Edmund Husserl, *Analyses Concerning Passive and Active Synthesis: Lectures on Transcendental Logic*, trans. Anthony J. Steinbock (Dordrecht/Boston: Kluwer Academic Publishers, 2001). See here particularly in reference to the discovery of the concept of "intentional drive": "Thus, we consider functions of affectivity that are founded purely in the *impressional sphere....* We may even allow *originally instinctive drive related preferences*" (ibid. 198; emphasis added).

10    Jacques Derrida, "Force and Signification," in *Writing and Difference*, trans. Alan Bass (Chicago: University of Chicago Press, 1978), 27; emphasis added. On this Husserlian deployment of the "drive" and its difference, in spite of many similarities with the Freudian perspective, see Rudolf Bernet, "Husserl sur les plaisirs d'un sujet charnel et pulsionnel," in *Force-pulsion-désir*, 299-331.

11    See on this point the justified remarks of Bruce Bégout, 'Pulsion et intention. Husserl et l'intentionnalité pulsionnelle," in Jean-Christophe Goddard, *La pulsion sous la direction de Jean-Christophe Goddard* (Paris: J. Vrin, 2006), 139-82. The fact remains that later phenomenology has not or only very little undertaken such a path of the drive, interpreting Husserl from his published works and not from the unpublished manuscripts which are now available, in particular Husserl, *Analyses Concerning Passive and Active Synthesis* [Husserliana, vol. XI].

12   *Writing and Difference*, 28; translation modified.

13   Maurice Merleau-Ponty, "The Philosopher and His Shadow," in *Signs*, 178. In regard to this analysis, I refer once again to my work "On the Edges of the Unconscious," Chapter Two, "A Phenomenology of the Underground: Maurice Merleau-Ponty," in *The Loving Struggle*, 66-69.

## Chapter Four: What is it?

1   Sigmund Freud, "The 'Uncanny' (1919)," in *The Standard Edition of the Complete Psychological Works of Sigmund Freud*, trans. James Strachey, vol. XVII (London: The Hogarth Press and the Institute of Psycho-analysis, 1991), 220.

2   Ibid., 241; translation modified.

3   Ibid.

4   Sigmund Freud, "Beyond the Pleasure Principle (1920)," in ibid., XVIII: 44.

5   Ibid., 16; emphasis added.

6   Bernet, *Force-pulsion-désir*, 261: "For us, the essential contribution of this book is at the level of the drives, that is to say, not beyond but below the pleasure principle."

7   Sigmund Freud, "The 'Uncanny' (1919)," in *The Standard Edition of the Complete Psychological Works of Sigmund Freud*, XVII, 205-10, citing 210.

8   Rather than *juxtaposing* the two examples (neuroses of war and children's play), we will instead see in them the *deepening* of the same phenomenon—the "compulsion to repeat"—but this time in the *enlarging* of the unique traumatic neuroses to psychic life as such. This is thus not the "abandonment" of one example in favor of another, except in the sense of abandonment as a passage or enlargement: "At this point I propose to abandon

[*verlassen*] the dark and dismal subject of the traumatic neurosis and pass on to examine the method of working employed by the mental apparatus in one of its earliest *normal* activities—I mean in children's play." Sigmund Freud, "Beyond the Pleasure Principle (1920)," in ibid., XVIII: 14; translation modified.

9    Ibid., 44.

10   Ibid., 38; translation lightly modified.

11   Jean-Paul Sartre, *Nausea*, trans. Lloyd Alexander (New York: New Directions Pub. Corp., 1969), 17; emphasis added.

12   Ibid.; emphasis added.

13   Charles de Bovelles, *Le livre du sage*, trans. Pierre Magnard (Paris: J. Vrin, 2010), ch. I, p. 27, v. 119.

14   Evagrius of Pontus, "The Monk: A Treatise on Practical Life," II.12 in *The Greek Ascetic Corpus*, trans. Robert E. Sinkewicz, Oxford Early Christian Texts (Oxford: Oxford University Press, 2003), 99; emphasis added. An account and a spirituality of acedia that is perfectly traced out (though Charles de Bovelles is not mentioned) can be found in Jean-Charles Nault, *La saveur de Dieu. L'acédie dans le dynamisme de l'agir* (Paris: les Éd. du Cerf, 2006).

15   Sigmund Freud, "Beyond the Pleasure Principle (1920)," in *The Standard Edition of the Complete Psychological Works of Sigmund Freud*, XVIII, 36. See also Rudolf Bernet's judicious commentary in *Force-pulsion-désir*, 269. He writes: "The drives behave, for Freud, in the manner of an elastic rubber band that when pulled automatically (and mechanically) returns to its original shape as soon as it is released… Being pulled involuntarily from a 'lifeless' state (*das Leblose*), the living wants to *return there*, and this return to the dead or to death constitutes their most fundamental and most powerful impulse."

16   Bernet, *Force-pulsion-désir*, 271.

## Chapter Five: It concerns me

[1]    Sigmund Freud, "The Ego and the Id (1923)," in *The Standard Edition of the Complete Psychological Works of Sigmund Freud*, trans. James Strachey, vol. XIX (London: The Hogarth Press and the Institute of Psycho-analysis, 1991), 12.

[2]    Ibid., 16-17; emphasis added.

[3]    Ibid., 23.

[4]    Ibid., 25; emphasis added. [Cap of hearing (*Hörkappe*) refers to the auditory lobe.]

[5]    Sigmund Freud, "Introductory Lectures on Psycho-Analysis (1916-1917 [1915-1917])," in *Complete Psychological Works*, XVI: 285.

[6]    Sigmund Freud, "The Ego and the Id (1923)," in ibid., XIX: 25. With Rudolf Bernet's remarkable commentary in *Force-pulsion-désir*, 362-365: "The ego behaves like a 'horseman of the Id' who holds a wild horse in a bridle in order to restrain its enthusiasm and to lead it the best he can without either spending too much energy or causing too much trouble... The ego thus strengthens the instinctual force of the Id by presenting it with trophies from its ancient hunts—returning this force, borrowed from the Id against the Id, in the sense of dominating it like a 'rider' who bridles his horse."

[7]    Freud, "The Ego and the Id (1923)," in *Complete Psychological Works*, XIX: 25.

[8]    He writes: "Speaking, *rather than 'letting be,'* solicits the Other. Speech cuts across vision." Levinas, *Totality and Infinity: An Essay on Exteriority*, 195; emphasis added.

[9]    Gilles Deleuze, *Nietzsche and Philosophy*, trans. Hugh Tomlinson, New ed. (London: Continuum, 2006), 38; emphasis added.

## Chapter Six: It touches me

1     Sigmund Freud, "New Introductory Lectures on Psycho-Analysis (1933 [1932])," in *The Standard Edition of the Complete Psychological Works of Sigmund Freud*, trans. James Strachey, vol. XXII (London: The Hogarth Press and the Institute of Psycho-analysis, 1986), 90; emphasis added.

2     See the first part "Descent into the Abyss," from my *The Wedding Feast of the Lamb*. See also the first chapter "*Khōra* or the Great Bifurcation: Jacques Derrida," and the second, "A Phenomenology of the Underground" (Merleau-Ponty), again from *The Loving Struggle*.

3     See lecture XXXI "The Dissection of the Psychical Personality," from "New Introductory Lectures on Psycho-Analysis (1933 [1932])," in *The Standard Edition of the Complete Psychological Works of Sigmund Freud*, XXII, 73.

4     Ibid.

5     See my essay "The Extra-Phenomenal."

6     Sigmund Freud, "New Introductory Lectures on Psycho-Analysis (1933 [1932])," in Freud, *The Standard Edition of the Complete Psychological Works of Sigmund Freud*, XXII, 80.

7     Ibid., 77.

8     Ibid., 79.

9     Ibid.

10     Ibid., 77.

11     See exergue p. 6.

12     Sigmund Freud, "New Introductory Lectures on Psycho-Analysis (1933 [1932])," in *The Standard Edition of the Complete Psychological Works of Sigmund Freud*, XXII, 79.

13    Ibid., 75.

14    Ibid., 79.

## Conclusion: What's God have to do with it?

1    Ibid., 75; translation modified; emphasis added.

2    Ibid.

3    Ibid., 75-6.

4    Ibid., 75.

5    Ibid., 78.

6    Ibid.

7    See the chapter "Is there a Drama of Atheist Humanism?" in my *The Metamorphosis of Finitude: An Essay on Birth and Resurrection*, trans. George Hughes (New York: Fordham University Press, 2012), 30-45.

8    See the chapter "*Khōra* or the Great Bifurcation: Jacques Derrida," and the section "The Lowly God" in the chapter "A Phenomenology of the Underground: Maurice Merleau-Ponty," in *The Loving Struggle*, 36-38 and 107-09.

9    Sigmund Freud, "Findings, Ideas, Problems," from "Shorter Writings (1937-1938)," in *The Standard Edition of the Complete Psychological Works of Sigmund Freud* XXIII: 300. For a psychoanalytic analysis of this concept see, P. L. Assoun, "Freud et la mystique," *La Nouvelle Revue de Psychanalyse* 22: 61. For a more theological treatment see Jean-Baptiste Lecuit, *L'anthropologie théologique à la lumière de la psychanalyse. La contribution majeure d'Antoine Vergote*, Cogitatio Fidei (Paris: les Éd. du Cerf, 2007), 411-12. (I thank the author and friend for pointing this out). I am here following Lecuit's translation of "self-apperception of the realm outside the self, of the id" and not "outside the self, the Id," which would make such a realm a sphere totally

independent of the Id as well as of the self, which does not make any sense either from a linguistic point of view or from a philosophical or theological point of view.

10    Isaiah 7:14: "Look, the young woman is with child and shall bear a son, and you shall name him Immanuel [*Imanou-El*] (God with us)." See the texts on "intertwining" from my aforementioned work, particularly the first section "Descent into the Abyss," in *The Wedding Feast of the Lamb*. See also the first chapter, "*Khōra* or the Great Bifurcation: Jacques Derrida," and "A Phenomenology of the Underground: Maurice Merleau-Ponty," in *The Loving Struggle*. See also "Une traversée du chaos (Dialogue avec Jérôme de Gramont)," in *Parcours d'embûches. S'expliquer. Disputationes: objections et réponses*, École Franciscaine de Paris (Paris: Éditions franciscaines de Paris, 2016).

## Epilogue: Regarding all of it

1    He writes: "Even if it were true, we do not believe the whole of philosophy to be worth one hour's effort" and also "Descartes useless and uncertain." Blaise Pascal, *Pensées and Other Writings*, trans. Honor Levi (Oxford: Oxford University Press, 1999), 30 and 105.

2    Emmanuel Falque and Sabine Fos-Falque, *Éthique du corps épandu, suivi de Une chair épandue sur le divan* (Paris: Cerf, 2018).

3    Maurice Merleau-Ponty, "Phenomenology and Psychoanalysis: Preface to Hesnard's *L'Œuvre de Freud*," in *The Essential Writings of Merleau-Ponty*, 86.

# Bibliography

Assoun, P.L. "Freud et la mystique." *La Nouvelle Revue de Psychanalyse* 22 (1980): 39-67.

Benson, Bruce Ellis and B. Keith Putt, eds. *Evil, Fallenness, and Finitude.* Cham, Switzerland: Palgrave Macmillan, 2017.

Bernet, Rudolf. *Force-pulsion-désir. Une autre philosophie de la psychanalyse. Problèmes et controverses.* Paris: J. Vrin, 2013.

Bovelles, Charles de. *Le livre du sage.* Translated by Pierre Magnard. Paris: J. Vrin, 2010.

Bruyeron, Roger. *1914. L'entrée en guerre de quelques philosophes. Edmund Husserl, Henri Bergson, Bertrand Russell, Sigmund Freud.* Paris: Hermann, 2014.

Deleuze, Gilles. *Nietzsche and Philosophy.* Translated by Hugh Tomlinson. New ed. London: Continuum, 2006.

Derrida, Jacques. *Writing and Difference.* Translated by Alan Bass. Chicago: University of Chicago Press, 1978.

Evagrius of Pontus. *The Greek Ascetic Corpus.* Translated by Robert E. Sinkewicz. Oxford Early Christian Texts. Oxford: Oxford University Press, 2003.

Falque, Emmanuel. *Crossing the Rubicon: The Borderlands of Philosophy and Theology.* Translated by Reuben Shank. New York: Fordham University Press, 2016.

———. "The Extra-Phenomenal." *Diakrisis: Yearbook of Theology and Philosophy* 1, no. 1 (May 2018): 9-28.

———. *The Loving Struggle: Phenomenological and Theological Debates.* Translated by Bradley B. Onishi and Lucas McCracken. Lanham: Rowman & Littlefield International, 2018.

———. *The Metamorphosis of Finitude: An Essay on Birth and Resurrection.* Translated by George Hughes. New York: Fordham University Press, 2012.

———. *Parcours d'embûches. S'expliquer. Disputationes: objections et réponses.* École Franciscaine de Paris. Paris: Éditions franciscaines de Paris, 2016.

———. *The Wedding Feast of the Lamb: Eros, the Body, and the Eucharist.* Translated by George Hughes. New York, NY: Fordham University Press, 2016.

Falque, Emmanuel, and Sabine Fos-Falque. *Éthique du corps épandu. Suivi de Une chair épandue sur le divan.* Paris: Cerf, 2018.

Fos-Falque, Sabine. *Comme en miroir. Les bruits de l'inconscient.* Paris: Cerf, 2018.

Freud, Sigmund. *The Standard Edition of the Complete Psychological Works of Sigmund Freud.* Translated by James

Strachey. Vol. XI, London: The Hogarth Press and the Institute of Psycho-analysis, 1986.

―――. *The Standard Edition of the Complete Psychological Works of Sigmund Freud.* Vol. XIV, London: The Hogarth Press and the Institute of Psycho-analysis, 1991.

―――. *The Standard Edition of the Complete Psychological Works of Sigmund Freud* Translated by James Strachey. Vol. XV, London: The Hogarth Press and the Institute of Psycho-analysis, 1991.

―――. *The Standard Edition of the Complete Psychological Works of Sigmund Freud.* Translated by James Strachey. Vol. XVI, London: The Hogarth Press and the Institute of Psycho-analysis, 1991.

―――. *The Standard Edition of the Complete Psychological Works of Sigmund Freud.* Translated by James Strachey. Vol. XVII, London: The Hogarth Press and the Institute of Psycho-analysis, 1991.

―――. *The Standard Edition of the Complete Psychological Works of Sigmund Freud.* Translated by James Strachey. Vol. XVIII, London: The Hogarth Press and the Institute of Psycho-analysis, 1991.

―――. *The Standard Edition of the Complete Psychological Works of Sigmund Freud.* Translated by James Strachey. Vol. XIX, London: The Hogarth Press and the Institute of Psycho-analysis, 1991.

―――. *The Standard Edition of the Complete Psychological Works of Sigmund Freud.* Translated by James Strachey. Vol. XXII, London: The Hogarth Press and the Institute of Psycho-analysis, 1986.

————. *The Standard Edition of the Complete Psychological Works of Sigmund Freud* Translated by James Strachey. Vol. XXIII, London: The Hogarth Press and the Institute of Psycho-analysis, 1991.

————, and Ernst Pfeiffer. *Sigmund Freud. Lou Andreas-Salomé. Briefwechsel* (Frankfurt a. M.): Fischer, 1966.

————, and Ernst Pfeiffer, and Lou Andreas-Salomé. *Sigmund Freud and Lou Andreas-Salomé: Letters*. Translated by William and Elaine Robson Scott. London: Hogarth Press and the Institute of Psycho-Analysis, 1972.

Goddard, Jean-Christophe. *La pulsion sous la direction de Jean-Christophe Goddard*. Paris: J. Vrin, 2006.

Groddeck, Georg. *The Book of the It: Psychoanalytic Letters to a Friend*. London: Daniel, 1935.

Heidegger, Martin. *Being and Time*. Translated by Joan Stambaugh. Albany, NY: State University of New York Press, 1996.

Henry, Michel. *The Essence of Manifestation*. Translated by Gerard Etzkorn. The Hague: Nijhoff, 1973.

————. *The Genealogy of Psychoanalysis*. Translated by Douglas Brick. Stanford, Calif.: Stanford University Press, 1993.

Husserl, Edmund. *Analyses Concerning Passive and Active Synthesis: Lectures on Transcendental Logic*. Translated by Anthony J. Steinbock. Dordrecht/Boston: Kluwer Academic Publishers, 2001.

————. *Cartesian Meditations: An Introduction to Phenomenology.* Translated by Dorion Cairns. The Hague: M. Nijhoff, 1960.

————. *Ideas Pertaining to a Pure Phenomenology and to a Phenomenological Philosophy: Second Book. Studies in the Phenomenology of Constitution.* Translated by Richard Rojcewicz and André Schuwer. Dordrecht/Boston: Kluwer Academic, 1989.

Janicaud, Dominique. *Phenomenology and the "Theological Turn": The French Debate.* Translated by Bernard G. Prusak. New York: Fordham University Press, 2000.

Jaspers, Karl, and Pierre Boudot. *Autobiographie Philosophique.* Translated by Pierre Boudot. Paris: Aubier, 1963.

Kahn, Laurence. *Faire parler le destin.* Paris: Klincksieck, 2005.

Lacan, Jacques. *The Ego in Freud's Theory and in the Technique of Psychoanalysis, 1954-1955.* Translated by Sylvana Tomaselli. *The Seminar of Jacques Lacan.* Vol. II. New York, N.Y.: W.W. Norton, 1988.

Lecuit, Jean-Baptiste. *L'anthropologie théologique à la lumière de la psychanalyse. La contribution majeure d'Antoine Vergote.* Cogitatio Fidei. Paris: les Éd. du Cerf, 2007.

Lévinas, Emmanuel. *Carnets de captivité et autres inédits, Œuvres I.* Paris: B. Grasset, 2009.

————. *Existence and Existents.* Translated by Alphonso Lingis. Dordrecht/London: Kluwer, 1988.

————. *Totality and Infinity: An Essay on Exteriority.* Translated by Alphonso Lingis. Pittsburgh: Duquesne University Press, 1969.

Lubac, Henri de. *Pic de la Mirandole. Études et discussions.* Paris: Aubier Montaigne, 1974.

Maldiney, Henri. *Maldiney. Une singulière présence.* Paris: Éditions les belles lettres, 2014.

Merleau-Ponty, Maurice. *Merleau-Ponty à la Sorbonne. Résumé de cours 1949-1952.* Grenoble: Cynara, 1988.

————. *The Essential Writings of Merleau-Ponty.* Translated by Alden L. Fisher. New York: Harcourt, Brace & World, 1969.

————. *The Merleau-Ponty Reader.* Edited by Ted Toadvine, and Leonard Lawlor. Evanston, Ill.: Northwestern University Press, 2007.

————. *Phenomenology of Perception.* Translated by Donald A. Landes. Abingdon, UK/New York: Routledge, 2012.

————. *The Prose of the World.* Translated by John O'Neill. Evanston, Ill.: Northwestern University Press, 1973.

————. *Signs.* Translated by Richard C. McCleary. Evanston, Ill.: Northwestern University Press, 1964.

————. *The Visible and the Invisible; Followed by Working Notes.* Translated by Alphonso Lingis. Evanston Ill.: Northwestern University Press, 1968.

Nault, Jean-Charles. *La saveur de Dieu. L'acédie dans le dynamisme de l'agir.* Paris: les Éd. du Cerf, 2006.

Nietzsche, Friedrich Wilhelm. *Thus Spoke Zarathustra.* Translated by Adrian Del Caro. Cambridge: Cambridge University Press, 2006.

Ouaknin, Marc-Alain. *Méditations érotiques. Essai sur Emmanuel Levinas.* Paris: Balland, 1992.

Pascal, Blaise. *Pensées and Other Writings.* Translated by Honor Levi. Oxford: Oxford University Press, 1999.

Ricœur, Paul. *The Conflict of Interpretations: Essays in Hermeneutics.* Edited by Don Ihde. Evanston Ill.: Northwestern University Press, 2007.

————. *Freud and Philosophy: An Essay on Interpretation.* Translated by Denis Savage. New Haven: Yale University Press, 1970.

Rosenzweig, Franz. *The Star of Redemption.* Translated by Barbara E. Galli. Madison, Wis.: University of Wisconsin Press, 2005.

Saint Aubert, Emmanuel de. *Vers une ontologie indirecte. Sources et enjeux critiques de l'appel à l'ontologie chez Merleau-Ponty.* Bibliothèque d'histoire de la philosophie temps modernes. Paris: J. Vrin, 2006.

Sartre, Jean-Paul. *Nausea.* Translated by Lloyd Alexander. New York: New Directions Pub. Corp., 1969.

# Index rerum

## A

acedia  58, 74-76, 117
animality  57, 63, 73, 99, 113
anorganic  17, 72-73, 77, 79-81, 96, 99-100
Aufklärung  21, 40, 109

## B

backlash  20, 28, 30, 32, 42, 63, 66, 90, 100, 105, 106
bestiality  57, 63, 73, 99, 113
body  15, 26, 27, 44, 60, 62, 64, 99
brutal  73
brutality  57-58, 63, 79, 81, 113

## C

cauldron  85-86, 93, 96
chaos  21, 35, 57, 64, 83, 85-86, 107
death  15, 17, 50, 52-57, 59-62, 70-77, 80, 83, 96, 112, 117

## D

disillusionment  51-53, 55-56, 59
drive  15, 17, 45, 46, 52-54, 56-58, 60-65, 66, 69-70, 72, 74-76, 79-81, 83, 86, 95, 115-117

**E**

ego   15, 17-18, 21, 32, 36-
37, 41, 46-47, 54-55, 57-
58, 60-61, 65, 69, 73, 77,
79-82, 86-90, 93-96, 108,
114-115, 118
elasticity   17, 76
Enlightenment   16, 21, 40-41,
45, 53-54, 100

**F**

flesh   43-44, 55, 62, 64, 110

**H**

horse   81-82, 89, 118

**I**

Id 15, 17-18, 21, 32, 36-37,
40-41, 47, 50, 55, 57-58,
59-66, 70, 73, 74, 77, 79-
83, 85-91, 93-97, 99-100,
104-105, 108, 113-114,
118, 120-121
inconceivable   50, 100

**K**

Körper   62

**L**

lapidary   74
Leib   62
life   17, 45, 53, 56-57, 61, 63,
70, 72, 73-74, 76-77, 80,
94, 100, 104-105, 109, 116
lifeless   73, 83, 93, 117
long road 19

**M**

magma   64, 66, 70, 73, 80, 88
meaning   15-17, 20, 30, 41,
50, 57, 59, 64, 73, 77, 87,
89, 108, 113-114
mineral   73-75, 77

**O**

obscurity   15, 29, 30, 37, 40,
43-44, 86
organic   17, 58, 60, 62, 64,
76, 77, 100

**P**

primitive   53, 57, 60, 88, 107
psychic   15, 18, 45, 58, 61-
62, 64, 77, 79, 81, 83, 86,
88-89, 100, 116

**R**

Rubicon   25-26, 90

## S

savagery  60
seeing  32, 42-45, 49, 59, 86
self  25, 32, 36-37, 41, 46, 52-
53, 54, 58, 60, 73-75, 90,
96, 105, 109, 113, 120-121
short cut  19
somatic 58, 60-64, 79, 83, 85
super-ego  15, 21, 36, 37, 79,
88, 95, 108
symbolic  58, 60, 62, 71, 72

## T

topography  15, 21, 37, 40,
44-45, 53, 60, 64, 79-81,
90, 104, 108
touching  15, 42-44, 110

## U

uncanny  18, 69-70, 81, 100
unconscious  15-16, 21, 30-31,
40, 44-45, 53-54, 60, 63,
66, 80, 101, 104-106, 108

## W

war  21, 28, 31, 40-41, 46-
47, 49-57, 59-60, 69-72,
79, 80-81, 95, 111, 113,
114, 116

# Index nominum

**A**
Andreas-Salomé 60

**B**
Bernet 63, 115-117, 123
Blanchot 105
Bovelles 74, 117, 123
Bruyeron 123

**D**
Deleuze 19, 26, 83, 118, 123
Derrida 19, 26, 35, 37, 66,
    77, 96, 100, 108, 115, 119-
    121, 123

**E**
Evagrius 74

**F**
Fos-Falque 109, 121, 124
Freud 19, 21, 24, 26, 29-32,
    35, 37, 40-52, 54-62, 69-75,
    80, 82-83, 85-90, 93-94,
    96, 100, 101, 103, 106-107,
    109, 111-114, 116-121,
    123-125, 127, 129

**G**
Goddard 115, 126
Gramont 121
Groddeck 31, 54, 55, 80, 108,
    113, 126

**H**

Heidegger 27-28, 31-32, 35, 43, 55, 61, 73, 114, 126

Henry 19, 26, 31, 100, 108, 126

Hesnard 16, 30, 33, 39, 103-105, 107, 109, 121

Husserl 27-29, 31, 32, 39, 46-47, 49, 62, 64-66, 106, 110-111, 115, 123, 126

**J**

Janicaud 104, 127

Jaspers 61, 114, 127

**L**

Lacan 60, 62, 63, 114, 127

Lecuit 120, 127

Lévinas 31-32, 43, 47, 64, 82, 103, 105, 110, 111, 113, 118, 127

Lubac 57, 73, 113, 128

**M**

Maldiney 37, 108, 128

Merleau-Ponty 18-20, 25-26, 28-33, 35, 37, 41-43, 45, 49, 62, 64, 66, 77, 88, 96, 100, 103, 105, 106-110, 116, 119, 120-121, 128-129

**N**

Nault 117, 128

Nietzsche 35, 46, 49, 55, 58, 64, 83, 113, 118, 123, 128

**O**

Ouaknin 110, 129

**P**

Pascal 99, 121, 129

Pico della Mirandola 57

**R**

Ricœur 19, 20, 23, 24, 29, 32, 100, 103, 106-107, 129

Rosenzweig 54-57, 112-113, 129

**S**

Saint Aubert 129

Sartre 74, 117, 129